Perspectives
The Multidisciplinary Series of
Physical Education and Sport Science

Volume 5

ASPECTS OF SPORT GOVERNANCE

ICSSPE

CIEPSS

International Council of Sport Science and Physical Education (ICSSPE)

Editors:	Darlene Kluka, William Stier, Jr. & Guido Schilling
Managing Editor:	Tamara Devine
Layout & Typesetting:	Tamara Devine
Cover Design:	axept, Berlin
	www.axeptdesign.de

*Board members until 2004

Perspectives
The Multidisciplinary Series of
Physical Education and Sport Science

Volume 5

ASPECTS OF SPORT GOVERNANCE

Edited by
Darlene Kluka, William Stier, Jr. & Guido Schilling

Meyer & Meyer Sport

British Library Cataloguing in Publication Data
A catalogue record for this book is available from the British Library

Aspects of Sport Governance/
Darlene Kluka / William Stier, Jr. / Guido Schilling (eds).
– Oxford : Meyer & Meyer Sport (UK) Ltd., 2005
(Perspectives – The Multidisciplinary Series of
Physical Education and Sport Science ; Vol.5)
ISBN 1-84126-132-7

© 2005 by Meyer & Meyer Sport (UK) Ltd
Adelaide, Auckland, Budapest, Graz, Johannesburg, New York,
Olten (CH), Oxford, Singapore, Toronto
Member of the World
Sportpublishers' Association
Managing Editor: Tamara Devine
Layout and Typesetting: Tamara Devine
Cover Design: axept, Berlin
Printed and bound by
FINIDR, s. r. o., Český Těšín
E-mail: verlag@m-m-sports.com
ISBN 1-84126-132-7

ASPECTS OF SPORT GOVERNANCE

CONTRIBUTING AUTHORS

Dr. Darlene Kluka is a Full Professor at Grambling State University of Louisiana, USA. She earned a BA at Illinois State University (ISU) in Health and Physical Education, an MA in Athletic Administration from ISU, and a Ph. D. in motor learning from Texas Woman's University. Since then, she has received numerous honors and awards. Some include the first ICHPER-SD Biennial Scholar in Sport and the Olympic Movement Award (1995), the NAGWS International Pathfinder Award (1999), the first AVCA Excellence in Education Award (1999), Louisiana AAHPERD Scholar Award (1999), Southern District AAHPERD Scholar Award (2001), and the Southern District AAHPERD Honor Award (2003). The Women's Sports Foundation has named an award in her honor: The Darlene A. Kluka Women's Sports and Activity Research Award (2000), and, most recently, the IAPESGW Kluka/Love Young Researcher Award was presented (2001). Presently, Kluka serves as a member of: the ICSSPE Editorial and Executive (as Treasurer) Boards; the Board of Consultants for IAPESGW; Charter member of the USA Volleyball Sports Medicine and Performance Commission. She has authored two texts, Volleyball (4th edition, 2000) and Motor Behavior: From Learning to Performance (2nd edition, 2005) and has served as Founding Co-Editor of the International Journal of Sports Vision (6 years). She is presently serving as Founding Editor of the International Journal of Volleyball Research (6 years). Her scholarly interests include visual perception and motor behavior, with particular regard for volleyball, women and sport, and the Olympic Movement. She has presented research and professional papers worldwide. She is an AAHPERD Research Fellow (1993) and an Honorary Research Fellow at the Hong Kong Baptist University's Research Center (1998).

Dr. William Stier, Jr's career has spanned 37 years during which he has served as a highly successful teacher, coach, and administrator. Distinguished Service Professor at the State University of New York, Brockport, he directs the undergraduate sport management and the graduate athletic administration programs where he also has responsibility for the coaching preparation program. At Brockport, he has been the athletics director and chair of the physical education and sport department. Stier has authored 15 books as well as 270 scholarly articles appearing in 76 different professional publications. He has served on editorial/advisory boards of 12 international and national scholarly journals. He is the current editor of The Physical Educator and the International Journal of Sport Management. Stier has made 146 presentations at international and national conventions and has conducted workshops and sport clinics in Hong Kong, Korea, Malaysia, Singapore, Mexico, St. Kitts-Nevis, China, Canada, and Greece. An AAHPERD Research Fellow, Dr. Stier had also been inducted into the Athletic Hall of Fame at Cardinal Stritch University, where he served as head basketball coach and athletic director.

Dr. Guido Schilling, retired, served as a lecturer in psychology and sport psychology at the Swiss Federal Institute of Technology in Zurich. He was a physical education teacher and earned his Ph.D. in Applied Psychology from Zurich University in 1967. He has taught at the Universities of Basel, Bern, Hamburg, and the Swiss Sport School in Magglingen. In addition to teaching, he has also been involved in the coaching and counseling of teams and elite athletes. He served as President of FEPSAC (Federation Europeenne de Psychologies des Sports et des Activites Corporelles) from 1975-1983. He has edited over 20 publications on sport science and sport psychology. In 1986, he was elected to the Executive Board of ICSSPE and served as Chair of ICSSPE's Editorial Board from 1998-2000. He has recently written a book on sport psychology and has contributed to CD ROMs involving sport psychology topics.

Ming Li is the Director of the School of Recreation and Sport Sciences at Ohio University and a Professor in Sports Administration. Li's teaching and research interests are in financial and economic aspects of sport, and international sport management. He received his bachelor's degree in education from Guangzhou Institute of Physical Culture (PRC), his master's degree in education from Hangzhou University (PRC), and his Doctor of Education from the University of Kansas in Sport Administration. He was the recipient of the 1999 Taylor Dodson Award given by the Southern District American Alliance for Health, Physical Education, Recreation and Dance. He has memberships on the editorial boards of four professional journals: (a) Journal of Sport Management, (b) International Journal of Sport Management, (c) Sport Marketing Quarterly, (d) International Sports Journal. For the contribution he made to his profession, the institution, and the community, he was given the 2000-2001 Award for Excellence in Service by Georgia Southern University. Li has published more than 20 articles in refereed journals, two books (i.e., Economics of Sport and Badminton Everyone), and three book chapters, and made numerous refereed presentations at state, national and international conferences.

Kristine Toohey is the Professor of Sport Management at Griffith University, Australia. Previously, she was on the faculty of the School of Leisure, Sport and Tourism, at The University of Technology, Sydney. She has also worked as a Program Manager for the Sydney Organising Committee for the Olympic Games. Her research and publishing focuses on the Olympic Games and politics in sport.

Dr. Tracy Taylor is an Associate Professor in Sport Management at the University of Technology, Sydney, Australia. She has over 20 years experience in teaching in the area of community sport and recreation. Tracy is actively involved in research, consultancy and community project work that encompasses dimensions of inclusively and diversity in sport, recreation and leisure. Her recent research and publications have focused on aspects of inclusionary service provision in sport and recreation and cultural diversity. Dr Taylor is also Course Director of the international Master of Management in Sport Management, a program delivered in Beijing in conjunction with Tsinghua University.

Peggy Kellers has a breadth of experience in athletics, sport psychology, and sport governance. Much of her 25-year career has been as a successful coach at the high school and university levels with experience in the sports of basketball, softball, and volleyball. She served for four years as the Executive Director of the National Association for Girls and Women in Sport. Peggy is a catcher in the Connecticut (1982) and National Softball Hall of Fame (1986). As an elite softball player she was an active player (1964-1974) when the first steps were taken towards softball becoming an Olympic sport. Prior to softball's first Olympic appearance in the 1996 Games, she was a specialty coach with USA Softball that trained and evaluated the catchers.

Dr. Chung Pak-kwong is currently the Director of Elite Training and Development of the Hong Kong Sports Development. He is responsible for overall management of resources and supervision of the Elite Training Program at the Hong Kong Sports Institute. Dr. Chung received his bachelor Degree in Physical Education from the National Taiwan Normal University and his Master and Doctoral Degrees in Physical Education from Springfield College, USA. He was the associate professor of the Department of Physical Education, Hong Kong Baptist University before taking up his current position in July 1998, where he had developed himself in the academic field, through teaching and conducting research in fitness and exercise psychology. Dr Chung was an all-round athlete. He captured twice the 1st runner-up positions at the Hong Kong Super Sportsman Competition held in 1981 and 1982. Other than sporting achievements, Dr. Chung has been promoting health and fitness to the general public for more than 20 years. He has published five books and numerous articles in local newspapers and magazines on topics of sports, fitness and health. He has also been a freelance sports commentator in a local television and broadcasting channel since 1983.

Sálmar Burger has an MBA with specialization in Sport Management from the University of Pretoria. Currently, he is a lecturer with the Department of Biokinetics, Sport and Leisure Sciences at the University of Pretoria. He previously held the positions of National Events Coordinator and National Office Supervisor with the South African Gymnastics Federation before joining the University. He is currently the technical vice-president of the Gauteng North Regional Gymnastics Association, and holds an international Brevet judges qualification from the International Gymnastics Federation (FIG). His research fields focus on sport management and specifically, governance in sport.

Prof. Anneliese Goslin received her doctorate from the University of Pretoria, South Africa on a training model for recreation managers in the South African sport and recreation industry. Since then she also obtained an MBA and has been instrumental in the founding and continuous development of under- and post- graduate programs in leisure management and sport management including an MBA (Sport Management) program at the University of Pretoria. She currently holds a full professorship in the Department of Biokinetics, Sport and Leisure Sciences at the University of Pretoria and is also the Director of the Center for Leisure Studies at the same university. Prof. Goslin is the President of Recreation South Africa (RECSA), the professional and scientific association for leisure sciences in South Africa. Her research interests are centered in sport management as well as leisure management and she was awarded the State President's Sport Award by the South African government for her services and initiatives in the South African sport and recreation industry.

Prof. Mollie Painter-Morland is currently Director of the Centre for Business and Professional Ethics and Associate Professor in the Department of Philosophy at the University of Pretoria, South Africa. She consults in the field of ethics management and corporate governance and specializes in the skills and knowledge needed to facilitate and manage ethical values in the workplace.

Prof. Dr. Mike McNamee is a member of the Centre for Philosophy, Humanities and Law in Health Care, in the School of Health Science at the University of Wales Swansea. He has co-edited several books in applied ethics and is editor for Routledge's book series, Ethics and Sport. He is a former President of the International Association for the Philosophy of Sport (IAPS), and is currently an executive member of the European College of Sport Science, the International Council of Sport Science and Physical Education (ICSSPE) and IAPS. He is the inaugural Chair of the British Philosophy of Sport Association. His most recent book is "Philosophy and the sciences of exercise, health and sport" (Routledge, 2004).

Scott Fleming is with the School of Sport and Leisure at the University of Gloucestershire. He is the author of 'Home and away': Sport and South Asian male youth (1995) and co-editor (with Alan Tomlinson) of Ethics, Sport and Leisure: Crises and Critiques (1997), and (with Ian Jones) of New Leisure Environments: Media, Technology and Sport (2002). His research interests include sport, leisure and ethnicity, 'fair play' and the ethics of corporate governance. He is currently the Chair of the Leisure Studies Association

Prof. Dr. Denise Jones is in the Department of Sport, Recreation and Exercise Science at the University of the Western Cape in South Africa. She lectures in the fields of Leisure Studies and Sports Management. Prof. Dr. Jones completed her PhD in Women and Sport at the Netherlands Research School for Women's Studies. She has received the South African National Sports Council's award for contribution to 'women and sport in South Africa'. Prof. Dr. Jones has served on various women and sports organizations and leisure studies committees. She has presented and published widely and written policies covering these areas. Her current research focus is on women, sport and health. Prof. Dr. Jones is a member of the Board of Consultants for the International Association of Physical Education and Sport for Girls and Women and is an Editorial Board member of the International Council for Sport Science and Physical Education.

Lionel Gilbert, M. S., earned his Bachelor of Science degree in health and physical education from Grambling State University of Louisiana. His Master of Science degree was earned in Sport Administration from Grambling State University. While there, he served as Parliamentarian for the Sport Leaders Association. He is presently employed as an instructor at Xavier University of New Orleans, Louisiana, USA.

Gretchen Ghent is a Librarian Emeritus at the University of Calgary, having taken early retirement after serving 25 years from staff librarian to her last position as Head of the Sciences/Professions Area in the University of Calgary Library. A founding member and currently the Chair of the North American Sport Library Network, she also is Vice-President for North America and Publications Officer for the International Association for Sports Information and a member of the Editorial Board of the International Council for Sport Science and Physical Education. Her website, Scholarly Sport Sites: a Subject Directory was created in 1999 to assist IASI, NASLIN and the academic community with links to important resources for sport sciences research. She was the main editor and a contributor to the ICSSPE publication, Perspectives, Vol. 4, Sport and Information Technology (2002) and contributes regularly to ICSSPE's Bulletin. She is currently the editor of NASLINE, the e-newsletter of the North American Sport Library Network and the IASI Newsletter.

FOREWORD

Mr. Adolf Ogi
SPECIAL ADVISOR TO THE
UNITED NATIONS SECRETARY GENERAL
ON SPORT FOR DEVELOPMENT AND PEACE

I congratulate the International Council for Sport Science and Physical Education (ICSSPE), and its leadership for its constant interest in the multi-faceted perspectives of the area of sport. The present volume, Perspectives: Sport Governance, explores a variety of topics that impact the present and future of sport worldwide. This is particularly relevant as the year 2005 was proclaimed the International Year of Sport and Physical Education (IYSPE 2005) by the UN-General Assembly.

During IYSPE 2005, we will have the unique opportunity to demonstrate the amazing value of sport for education, health, development and peace. The many benefits of sport and physical activity should not only be enjoyed by the individual, but also felt throughout society. There is therefore, a crucial need for all members of the international family of sport and for all their partners to understand that in the future ethics will be a very important issue. In my view ethical behavior represents respect, such as respect for the environment, for diversity and "others" in general. Respect can be learned through the practice of sport. Sport can help build a culture of peace and tolerance by bringing people together on common ground, across national and other boundaries to promote understanding and mutual respect.

Sport is an ideal school of life because sport teaches us the essential lessons such as respect for the opponent, for the rules and for the referee. Sport teaches us that victory is ephemeral and how to overcome defeat with dignity and to manage the euphoria of victory. It teaches us to integrate into a team and that to reach victory it takes regular and often hard training. International sport events with their spirit of fair and peaceful competition bridge religions, race and social and cultural divides. They provide us with examples for the positive power of sport, which reaches far beyond the athletic arena, the ski track or the football stadium.

The fundamental principles of sport – respect for opponents and for rules, teamwork and fairplay – are consistent with the United Nations Charter. During the past decade relations between the United Nations and civil society have grown in every respect. Relations with the sports world have reflected this trend. Numerous sports organizations have concluded cooperation agreements with a number of United Nations programs and funds and have lent their support to UN efforts in the field. Acknowledging the growing potential of these partnerships, in 2001 the UN-Secretary-General Kofi Annan created a novel mandate and appointed me as his Special Adviser on Sport for Development and Peace.

My mandate is oriented not only towards the world of sport, sports industries and governments, but also towards the UN-system. It includes the following duties within the UN: consulting with agencies of the United Nations system engaged in development, peace-making and peace-building, and identifying the tasks and programs that might benefit from the involvement of sports organizations to achieve their objectives.

With these aims in mind, the United Nations Inter-Agency Task Force on Sport for Development and Peace was formed, bringing together agencies with significant experience using sport in their work, including ILO, UNESCO, WHO, UNDP, UNV, UNEP, UNHCR, UNICEF, UNODC and UNAIDS*. The Task Force sought to crystallize the lessons learned from the growing experience within the United Nations system of using sport as a tool for development and peace, as well as to seize the growing interest by the world of sport in United Nations activities.

Several concrete steps have been taken in recent years in support of the use of sport for development and peace. Similarly, in the sports world, various sports federations and organizations have demonstrated an increasing awareness about the broader potential of sport.

However, much more should be done. The collective commitment to the creation of a worldwide sport governance environment that promotes ethical decision making, where differences are respected and valued, is pivotal for those who will be touched by sport governance. Such ethical behavior is assessed based upon systemic thinking and vision, integrity, courage, commitment, discipline, persistence, durability, capacity building and human development, teamwork, communication, and the pursuit of excellence. Therefore, I strongly approve the initiative taken by the ICSSPE to fully dedicate this publication to the topic of the Aspects of Sport Governance.

*ILO – International Labor Organization, UNESCO – United Nations Educational, Scientific and Cultural Organization, WHO – World Health Organization, UNDP – United Nations Development Program, UNV – United Nations Volunteers, UNEP – United Nations Environment Program, UNHCR – United Nations High Commission for Refugees, UNICEF – United Nations International Children's Fund, UNODC – United Nations Office on Drugs and Crime and UNAIDS – Joint United Nations Program on HIV/AIDS.

PREFACE

Darlene Kluka, William Stier (Jr), Guido Schilling

Over the past decade there has been a surge in publications involving components of sport administration and management. One of the most important, yet least documented components, is sport governance. This volume of Perspectives is dedicated to providing a unique look into the topic of sport governance. Sport Governance has been defined as a relatively new discipline that is based in sport and management science. A contemporary definition was presented by Hums and MacLean (2004) as "…the exercise of power and authority in sport organization, including policy making, to determine organizational mission, membership, eligibility, and regulatory power within the organization's appropriate local, national, or international scope". (p. 5)

The International Council of Sport Science and Physical Education (ICSSPE), through its leadership, has determined a long-term publications strategic plan to ensure success of endeavors such as this. Five years ago, members of the ICSSPE's Editorial Board envisioned a profound opportunity to expand the global knowledge bases on a variety of topics from a multidisciplinary perspective. The readership of the publication is as diverse as the content. Individuals representing governmental and nongovernmental sport and sport science organizations, sport federations, universities and research institutes may benefit from this volume of Perspectives. Representatives from the International Olympic Committee (IOC), UNESCO, WHO, World Federation of the Sporting Goods Industry (WFSGI), and the General Assembly of International Sports Federations (GAISF) may also find it useful. Moreover, those with an interest in sport governance, including teachers, coaches, and sport scientists, may also apply its contents toward the development of future leaders.

The volume has been divided into three sections: International Olympic Committee/International Perspectives; Sports Federations; and Ethics and Leadership.   The first section provides the reader with insights into the International Olympic Committee (Li), National Olympic Committees (Taylor) and the 1980 and 1984 Olympic Games Boycotts (Toohey).

The second section, Sports Federations, presents perspectives involving a personal perspective on the International Softball Federation (Kellers), elite sport development and national team selection in Hong Kong (Chung), and compliance with best practice governance systems by national sports federations in South Africa (Burger, Goslin & Painter-Morland).

The third section, Ethics and Leadership, completes the Perspectives volume.   The ethics of corporate governance in sport: theory, method and operationalization (McNamee & Fleming), sport, culture and difference (Jones), and from the boardroom: parliamentary procedures (Kluka & Gilbert) provide readers with underpinnings of the framing of governance.

The volume concludes with an outstanding appendix, which includes Internet resources (Ghent), book and article resources (Stier), and an assessment tool for sport governance compliance (Burger).   In addition, examples of Declarations and Recommendations are included to show documentation that can be used to structure and direct action within relevant organizations.   Guiding documents such as these can support good governance practices within an organization.   The progression of Women in Sport shows how development can occur, with refinement and addition made to documents over time.

As editors, it is our perspective that sport governance success is inspired by those working collectively to accomplish a mission. Our collective commitment to the creation of a worldwide sport governance environment in which people can do their best, where missions and goals can be ethically achieved, where differences are respected and valued, and where behaviors are assessed based upon systematic thinking and vision, integrity, courage, commitment, discipline, persistence, durability, leadership development, teamwork, communication, and the pursuit of excellence is pivotal for those whose responsibility is sport governance.

References

Hums, M.A. & MacLean, J.C. (2004). *Governance and policy in sport organizations.* Scottsdale, Arizona: Holcomb Hathaway, Publishers.

INTERNATIONAL OLYMPIC COMMITTEE

Ming Li

The International Olympic Committee (IOC) is an international non-governmental, non-profit organization, founded in 1894 by Baron Pierre de Coubertin to revive the Ancient Greek Olympic Games and promote the cause commonly known as the Olympic Movement. As the Olympic Charter states, "the International Olympic Committee is the supreme authority of the Olympic Movement" (International Olympic Committee, 2000, p. 10). As such, the IOC owns all rights to the Olympic symbols, flag, motto, anthem and Olympic Games (i.e., the Games of the Summer Olympiad and the Olympic Winter Games). The term "Olympiad" designates a period of four successive years.

The mission of the IOC is several-fold, including (a) to promote high performance sport and sport for all; (b) to ensure the regular celebration of the Olympic Games; and (c) to promote women in sport and sports ethics; and (d) to protect athletes. Supervision of the organization of the Olympic Games is the primary responsibility of the IOC.

The Olympic Movement and Its Membership
The Olympic Movement is a phrase that the IOC uses to promote a cause whose goal is

> "to contribute to building a peaceful and better world by educating youth through sport practiced without discrimination of any kind and in Olympic spirit, which requires mutual understanding with a spirit of friendship, solidarity and fair play" (International Olympic Committee, 2000, p. 9).

Correspondence to: Ming Li, School of Recreation and Sport Sciences, Grover Center E160, Ohio University, Athens, Ohio 45701, U.S.A. Email: Mingli@ohio.edu

To achieve this goal, the Olympic Movement is engaged in a variety of activities, which include

1. Promoting sport and competitions through the intermediary of national and international sports institutions, worldwide.
2. Cooperating with public and private organizations to place sport at the service of mankind.
3. Assisting the development of "Sport for All".
4. Promoting the advancement of women in sport at all levels and in all structures, with a view to achieving equality between men and women.
5. Opposing all forms of commercial exploitation of sport and athletes.
6. Fighting against doping.
7. Promoting sports ethics and fair play.
8. Raising awareness of environmental problems.
9. Providing financial and educational support for developing countries through the IOC institution called Olympic Solidarity. (International Olympic Committee, 2003).

The membership of the Olympic Movement includes organizations, athletes and other persons who agree to be guided by the Olympic Charter (International Olympic Committee, 2000). Specifically, it consists of the International Olympic Committee, the National Olympic committees (NOCs) of individual nations, the International Sporting Federations (IFs) of various sports recognized by the IOC, the Organizing Committees of the Olympic Games (OCOGs), athletes, judges and referees, associations and clubs, as well as all organizations and institutions recognized by the IOC, such as continental associations of NOCs (e.g., Pam-American Sports Organizations, Olympic Council of Asia, etc.) (Buchanan & Mallon, 2001). Any organization that wishes to become affiliated with the Olympic Movement, must first agree to abide by the Olympic Charter. They may then receive recognition from the IOC, which has been granted the supreme authority of the Olympic Movement.

The International Olympic Committee and Its Membership

According to the Olympic Charter (2000), the International Olympic Committee is composed of a maximum of 115 co-opted members. That number may rise to 130. The IOC members meet in the IOC Session at least once every year.

The elected IOC members act as the IOC's representatives in their respective countries, not as delegates of their country within the IOC (International Olympic Committee, 2000). Once an IOC member turns seventy, he or she must retire at the end of that calendar year, unless their election to the IOC took place before the opening of the 110th Session (i.e., December 11, 1999). Without exception, an IOC member must retire at the age of eighty. The IOC Nominations Committee identifies and recommends qualified candidates to the IOC Session when vacancies are anticipated and the IOC Session then chooses its new members from among those recommended. All individuals involved in the Olympic Movement have the right to be nominated and elected to the membership of IOC (International Olympic Committee, 2000).

The IOC membership includes active athletes and presidents of IFs and NOCs. There are currently 126 members, 21 Honorary members and 4 Honor members (International Olympic Committee, 2003). An IOC member who "retires after serving the IOC for at least ten years and having rendered exceptional services to it" may be awarded the "honorary member" title and honor members are given to individuals outside the IOC who "have rendered particularly outstanding services to" the IOC (International Olympic Committee, 2000, p. 28). Neither Honorary members nor Honor members have voting privileges. Juan Antonio Samaranch is Honorary President for life.

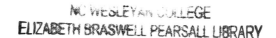

The Governance Structure of the IOC

THE IOC SESSION

The IOC Session is a general meeting of all members of the IOC, held at least once a year. At the meeting, IOC members adopt, modify and interpret the Olympic Charter, and elect new IOC members as well as its President and Executive Board members (International Olympic Committee, 2000). In the Olympic year, the IOC Session is usually held immediately prior to the Olympic Games or the Olympic Winter Games, in the host city. Special sessions may be called by either the IOC president or by written request of no less than one third of the IOC members. It is the supreme organ and the major rule-making body of the IOC (Buchanan & Mallon, 2001; International Olympic Committee, 2000).

THE EXECUTIVE BOARD

The Executive Board consists of the IOC President, four Vice-presidents and ten other members who are elected by the IOC Session for a four-year term. It is recommended that its members come from various segments of the Olympic Movement, such as NOCs, IFs, and athletes. The Executive Board meets when convened by the President on the latter's initiative or at the request of the majority of its members (International Olympic Committee, 2000).

The Executive Board is responsible for running the IOC effectively. Specifically, it:

1. attends to the observance of the Olympic Charter;
2. assumes the ultimate responsibility for the administration of the IOC;
3. approves the IOC's internal organization, its organization chart and all internal regulations relating to its organization;
4. is responsible for the management of the IOC's finances and prepares an annual report;
5. presents a report to the Session on any proposed change of rule or bye-law;

6. submits to the IOC Session the names of the persons whom it recommends for election to the IOC;
7. conducts the procedure for acceptance and selection of candidatures for the organization of the Olympic Games;
8. creates and allocates IOC honorary distinctions;
9. establishes the agenda for the IOC Sessions;
10. appoints the Director General and Secretary General upon receiving a proposal from the President;
11. keeps the records of the IOC;
12. enacts, in the form it deems most appropriate, (codes, rulings, norms, guidelines, guides, instructions) all regulations necessary to ensure the proper implementation of the Olympic Charter and the organization of the Olympic Games;
13. performs all other duties assigned to it by the Session. (International Olympic Committee, 2000, p. 38-39)

The President of the IOC presides over the Executive Board. With the exception of the President, who serves an initial term of eight years, the four Vice-presidents and ten other members all serve a four-year term beginning at the end of the Session which elected them, and terminating at the end of the last ordinary Session during the year in which their terms expire (International Olympic Committee, 2000). In order to be re-elected to serve such office again, the Vice-presidents and ten other board members must sit out for a minimum four-year interim. However, they are exempted from this rule if elected either as President or Vice-president (International Olympic Committee, 2000).

If the President is unable to fulfill the duties of his or her office, the Vice-president, who is senior in such office, replaces him or her until a new President is elected at the next IOC Session. This new President will complete the term of office of the President whom he or she replaces. In the case that a Vice-president position is vacant, the vacancy will be filled at the following IOC Session, and the Vice-president thus elected holds office until the term of the Vice-president he or she is replacing expires. He or she is immediately eligible for any office on the Executive Board. The replacement of a member of the Executive Board follows the same procedure used to fill the office of a Vice-president (International Olympic Committee, 2000).

THE PRESIDENT

IOC members elect the President of the IOC by secret ballot for an initial term of eight years, renewable once for four years. Jacques Rogge, of Belgium, is the current President. He was elected to the IOC presidency at the 112th Session on July 16, 2001 (International Olympic Committee, 2003).

In addition to acting as the permanent representative of the IOC, the President also presides over all activities of the organization. The activities include, but are not limited to, setting up or dissolving permanent or ad hoc IOC commissions and working groups.

IOC ADMINISTRATION

The IOC Administration is the administrative arm of the IOC. It prepares, implements and follows up the decisions of various rule-making bodies of the IOC, such as the Session, the Executive Board, and the President on a day-to-day basis. Specifically, it is responsible for:

1. Preparing and following up the work of all IOC commissions;
2. Serving as a permanent liaison with the IFs, NOCs and OCOGs (Organizing Committee of the Olympic Games);
3. Coordinating the preparation for all Olympic Games;
4. Organizing and preparing other Olympic events;
5. Circulating information within the Olympic Movement;
6. Advising candidate cities;
7. Maintaining relations with international governmental and non-governmental organizations dealing with, in particular, sport, education and culture;
8. Serving as a liaison with Olympic Solidarity;
9. Completing other tasks of an ongoing or ad hoc nature assigned to it by the President and the Executive Board. (International Olympic Committee, 2003).

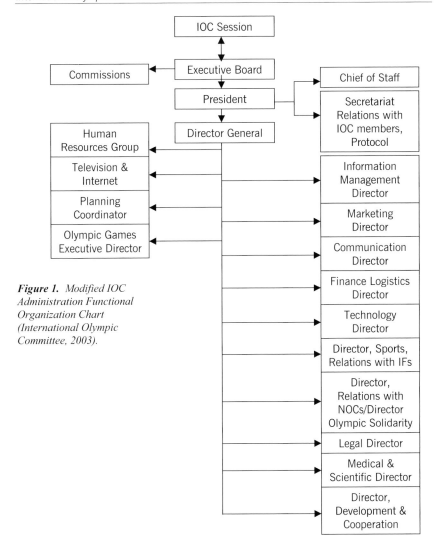

Figure 1. *Modified IOC Administration Functional Organization Chart (International Olympic Committee, 2003).*

The IOC administration is headed by the Director General who reports directly to the President. Under the Director General are Directors of many departments responsible for dealing with business in a specific area of Olympic operations, such as International Cooperation, Olympic Games Coordination, Relations with IFs, NOCs and OCOGs, Finance, Marketing, Legal Affairs, Technology, Control and Coordination of operations, Communications, and Medical. Figure 1 is a simplified flow chart of IOC Administration (International Olympic Committee, 2003).

IOC COMMISSIONS
To deal with specific issues related to the Olympic Movement, the IOC has created many commissions (Buchanan & Mallon, 2001). As aforementioned, it is directly under the purview and authority of the President of the IOC to create and dissolve any IOC commission. The President charges each commission with certain responsibilities. For example, the Athletes' Commission's responsibilities include (a) discuss its views biannually with the IOC Executive Board and report to the IOC Session, (b) delegate athlete representatives to other IOC Commissions, and (c) establish working groups to act as liaison to the OCOGs (International Olympic Committee, 2003). Currently, there are 17 major commissions, including Athletes' Commission, Commission for Culture and Olympic Education, Coordination Commission for the Olympic Games, Ethics Commission, Evaluation Commission for the XXI Olympic Winter Games in 2010, Marketing Commission, Medical Commission, Olympic Games Study Commission, Olympic Philately, Numismatic and Memorabilia Commission, Olympic Program Commission, Olympic Solidarity, Press Commission, Radio and Television Commission, Sport and Environment Commission, Sport for All Commission, TV and Internet Rights Commission, and Women and Sport Working Group.

References

Buchanan, I. & Mallon, B. (2001). *Historical Dictionary of the Olympic Movement*. (2nd Edition). Lanham, Maryland: The Scarecrow Press.

International Olympic Committee. (2000). *Olympic Charter*. Lausanne, Switzerland: International Olympic Committee.

International Olympic Committee. (2003). *Organization*. Retrieved July 15, 2003, from http://www.olympic.org/uk/organisation/index_uk.asp

NATIONAL OLYMPIC COMMITTEES

Kristine Toohey

Introduction

While the International Olympic Committee (IOC) is the supreme authority of the Olympic Movement, there are a number of other entities, which, together with athletes, officials and sponsors, comprise the 'Olympic Family'. Their governance, as it relates to the celebration of the Olympic Games, is determined by the procedures articulated by the IOC in *the Olympic Charter*. Examples of such organizations include: the International Federations (IFs) of sports which conduct competitions in either the Summer or Winter Olympic Games; and the Organizing Committees of the Olympic Games (OCOGs). A third category of organizations, which also belong to the Olympic Movement, is comprised of the National Olympic Committees (NOCs) (Toohey and Veal, 2000).

Senn (1999, p.11) describes NOCs as 'the basic building blocks in the structure of the Olympic Games. They are the organizations that select, supervise and certify the Olympic competitors. Without certification from an NOC no athlete can compete.' However, this ruling, like many other IOC regulations, can been circumvented when it suits the purposes of the IOC, for example, in 1992, when individual Yugoslav athletes were allowed to compete in the Barcelona Games and also in 2000 when individual East Timorese athletes were invited to participate in the Sydney Games, although neither country, at those points in time, had an NOC to endorse its athletes. Athletes too, have sought to overturn this ruling of certification, when seeking to have the Court of Arbitration of Sport reach a decision to compel their NOC to include them in their Olympic team.

Correspondence to: Professor Kristine Toohey, Department of Tourism, Leisure, Hotel and Sport Management, Griffith University, PMB 50, Gold Coast Mail Centre, Qld. 9726, Australia

Two recent, but unsuccessful, examples of this include Emma Carney's appeal for a place on the 2000 Australian Olympic triathlon team and slalom skier Jono Brauer attempt to be included in the 2002 Australian team for the Salt Lake City Winter Olympic Games.

To be designated as an NOC requires IOC endorsement. According to the *Olympic Charter* (2001, p.51), 'this recognition can only be granted to an organization, the jurisdiction of which coincides with the limits of the country in which it is established and has its headquarters.' In 2002 there were 199 such National Olympic Committees. (see Table One) They are spread over the five continents and presently number more than the member states of the United Nations. Although most NOCs are from nations, the IOC also recognizes NOCs from independent territories, commonwealths, protectorates, and geographical areas.

Politics
The IOC asserts that there can be only one NOC per country, however it has also ignored this rule in recent times when it has suited its purpose, for example, its admission of Palestinian athletes at the 1996 Atlanta Summer Olympic Games (Senn, 1999).

Earlier, protracted disputes about recognition of German and Chinese NOCs had created some of the IOC's most protracted political problems. Both problems began before the 1952 Helsinki Games and continued to fester for decades.

Germany had a long-established NOC before World War II. After the war, because of the Allied division of the country, the nation was split into two. National Olympic Committees were formed in both the new East and West Germanys. In 1949 each of these rival states had only received official recognition from a smattering of countries and neither from the United Nations. Both committees approached the IOC for official recognition. Because of the abovementioned IOC policy of acknowledging only one NOC per country, the matter needed to be resolved and, like so many other issues, the political situation of the time drove the issue and similarly, the IOC's response to it.

In 1950 the IOC voted to give provisional recognition to the West German Committee. A year later this NOC received full IOC recognition, although the Soviets insisted that, as there were two states, there should be two separate committees. The debate over recognition for a separate East German NOC continued and, reflecting the general Cold War relations, was at times acrimonious. As an early compromise, the IOC drew up an agreement whereby the two sides would attempt to form a single team for the 1952 Helsinki Games. At this stage the East Germans refused this concession, and as a result, no East Germans participated at these Games. However, by 1956, the two Germanys entered a single team in both the Summer and Winter Olympics. While a strict interpretation of IOC rulings was not applied through this solution, it can be easily argued that the outcome was far more positive for the competing athletes, especially those from the East. It was not until the 1972 Olympics (held ironically in Munich, the Federal Republic of Germany (West Germany) that the East German NOC (now fully recognized by the IOC as the NOC from the German Democratic Republic) fielded its own team at an Olympic Games and continued to do so for the term of the country's existence (Warning, 1980).

Similar to the recognition problem with the Germans was another problem for the IOC of whether to recognize the NOC from the Peoples' Republic of China (Communist China) or Nationalist China (also known as Taiwan or Formosa). China, like Germany, had an NOC before the Second World War. After the communist takeover in 1949, all of its NOC committee members had fled to Taiwan and continued to maintain an NOC, claiming jurisdiction over Olympic sport throughout all of China and retaining its name of the Chinese Olympic Committee. This committee continued to receive recognition from the IOC. Meanwhile, on the mainland, the communist government had created an All China Athletic Federation to adjudicate sports bodies in its territory. Although not an NOC, this federation affiliated with a number of IFs that had previously recognized the Chinese NOC and which were themselves approved by the IOC (Warning, 1980).

As, officially, there should not be two Chinese teams, the IOC had to reach a decision as to which of the organizations would field an Olympic team for the Helsinki Games. Twenty-two IOC members voted for neither team to be invited and twenty-nine for both. The IOC President, Avery Brundage, 'acknowledged that the IOC was breaking its own rules by allowing participation by a territory without an NOC, but argued that the circumstances were exceptional' (Hill, 1996, p.45). A compromise was finally reached, whereby both committees would be invited to compete in only the sports in which they had been recognized by the IFs. This proposal, while acceptable to both the IOC and the Helsinki Organizing Committee did not find favor with the Nationalist Chinese who withdrew their single competitor. The Peoples' Republic of China team arrived in Helsinki too late to compete in their scheduled events. Consequently, there were no Chinese competitors in the 1952 Games (Warning, 1980).

After four more years of intense political posturing and threats of non-participation at the 1956 Games, the issue had not been resolved, despite the fact that in 1954 the IOC had recognized the People's Republic of China NOC (known as the 'Olympic Committee of the Chinese Republic' and in 1957 as the 'Olympic Committee of the People's Democratic Republic of China'). Later in that year, both Chinese NOCs were invited to send teams to compete in the Melbourne Olympic Games. However, Melbourne saw only athletes from Nationalist China compete, and their visit was not without incident. At the official opening of the Olympic Village on 29 October 1956, Australian Army Corporal, Brian Agney, inadvertently raised the flag of the Peoples' Republic of China instead of the flag of Nationalist China. "I didn't know the difference in the flags," Corporal Agney apologized, "but I certainly do now" (Phinzy in Warning, 1980).

In 1959, following continued pressure from the communist bloc, the IOC proposed that the NOC from Taiwan would have to change its name. This was duly altered to the 'Olympic Committee of the Republic of China', however, their 1960 team was forced to compete at the Rome Games as Taiwan (Formosa). At the Opening Ceremony, the team resourcefully expressed its displeasure at this ruling when the placard bearer, when passing the official stand, briefly showed a sign saying 'under protest' and then quickly replaced it (Warning, 1980).

The question of Chinese participation continued to be a thorn in the Olympic side and an opportunity for political point scoring for politicians from both the East and West. There was ever only one of the two Chinas competing at a Games until the 1984 Los Angeles Olympic Games, when, for the first time, both of China's NOCs sent teams. The issue was so divisive that, in 1976, in addition to its other boycott problems, the IOC voted on canceling the Montreal Games, when the Canadian government refused to allow the Taiwanese team to use the name 'China', in its title, raise its flag or play its anthem. The Taiwanese left the day before the Games began (Hill, 1996). In 1980 neither country competed.

The recognition of Chinese and German NOCs are examples of how international disputes are played out in the Olympic arena.

On a number of other occasions, the IOC has also taken the initiative to use its Olympic Charter rulings to exclude nations from sending teams to compete at the Games. In 1996 it refused Eritrea admission to the Atlanta Games, as it had not recognized an Eritrean National Olympic Committee. In 2000 Afghani athletes could not compete at the Sydney Olympics as the IOC had withdrawn recognition of Afghanistan's National Olympic Committee. According to Hill (1994, p. 1):

> 'It might be thought that for the International Olympic Committee… to give recognition to a new…NOC, or to withhold it, would be no more important than any other decision by keen sportspeople about whether or not to compete with one another. However, the decision to recognize an NOC contributes to the far more important decision as to whether a territory with aspirations to recognition as a state (like East Germany after the Second World War) is to achieve it, or whether a country like South Africa, whose internal policies have been widely reviled, should continue to enjoy normal relations with other states. In such cases, governments use sport as a weapon.'

While the IOC requests the NOCs to 'maintain harmonious and cooperative relations with appropriate bodies' it believes that the NOCs should 'preserve their autonomy and resist pressures of any kind, including those of a political... nature' (IOC, 2001, p. 49). In other words, in principle, the IOC considers that NOCs should be independent of government and the *Olympic Charter* (2001, p. 51) expressly notes that 'governments or other public authorities shall not designate any members of an NOC. However, an NOC may decide, at its discretion, to elect as members representatives of such authorities'. However, understandably, the reality is far removed from this ideal.

Some politicians and governments are heavily involved in their nation's NOC membership, policymaking and funding functions. Even nations, such as the United States, which do not subsidize their Olympic teams, have effectively prevented their NOC from competing at a Games, while other Western countries, such as Australia and Great Britain have also, albeit unsuccessfully, attempted to prevent their NOC from attending an Olympic competition. (For a more detailed account of these examples, see the Olympic Boycott Chapter by Taylor in this volume). Thus, like all other aspects of the Olympic Games, the NOCs are subject to political interference.

Mission of the National Olympic Committees
While the size, solvency and power of the 199 NOCs varies markedly, they all have a number of common characteristics, one of which is their raison d'etre. According to the IOC website (www.olympic.org), their mission is to 'propagate the fundamental principles of Olympism at a national level within the framework of sports activity'. To achieve this mission they have a number of aims and objectives. These include:
- Promoting the fundamental principles of Olympism at a national level within the framework of sports
- Ensuring the observance of the Olympic Charter in their country
- The development of athletes and support for the development of sport for all programs and high performance sport in their country
- Training of sports administrators by organizing educational programs
- Committing themselves to taking action against discrimination and violence in sport

- Fighting against the use of substances and procedures prohibited by the IOC or IFs
- Ensuring that athletes from their respective nations attend the Olympic Games
- Supervising the preliminary selection of potential bid cities. (Before a candidate city can compete against those in other countries, it first must win the selection process by the NOC in its own country. The National Olympic Committee can then name that city to the IOC as a candidate to host the Olympic Games.)

Obviously the day-to-day functioning and funding of the NOCs varies significantly. Some NOCs, such as the United States Olympic Committee (USOC) and the Australian Olympic Committee (AOC), are relatively large, permanently staffed organizations, backed by strong financial assets and are located in affluent Olympic markets. Because of this they are better placed to further their advantage. For example, while funds from IOC Olympic marketing programs help defray costs (including the training and development of athletes and the cost of sending Olympic teams to the Games) for all NOCs, the USOC 'wrangled particularly good deals from the IOC because United States (US) networks and corporations put so much into IOC coffers. The USOC gets nearly half the $406 million that the IOC funnels to nations, leaving other countries to jockey for the rest' (Abrahamson and Wharton, 2000:
http://apse.dallasnews.com/contest/2000/writing/over250.enterprise.first2.asp).

The inequity between large and small NOCs is even greater when it comes to the division of the spoils of the IOC's corporate sponsorship program. According to Abrahamson and Wharton (2000): 'the USOC alone gets $US 80 million over four years, while the other Olympic nations must share roughly the same amount. For 140 "small" nations, such as Cambodia and Mongolia, the IOC provides $US 40,000 each. Of the "big" countries, 56 get between $US 50,000 and $US 5 million; the two nations hosting the Games get a special share.'

In addition, Olympic host NOCs also can receive added windfalls from the profits that an OCOG makes from staging Games. The AOC earned $A91 million from the Sydney 2000 Olympic Games. Even before this, in 1993, its investment portfolio of $A17 million had permitted it to take a gamble and invest in a casino in Cairns, on the Great Barrier Reef. Gordon (1994, p. 435) notes that this 'kind of involvement ... would have been unthinkable a decade or so before, on both ethical and financial grounds'.

However, not all, or even most, NOCs are financially secure. Some NOCs are so cash strapped that they have no permanent employees or internet access, a service that is taken for granted in the first world. This lack of computer technology and the human resources to access it makes prompt communication between the IOC and all of its NOCs imperfect. In a world where speed of information exchange is becoming commonplace and even a necessity, this divide between the 'have' and 'have not' NOCs can be problematic.

The Association of National Olympic Committees

The relationship between the IOC and the NOCs has not always been harmonious. In the 1960s, believing that the IOC leadership was not properly acknowledging their contribution and importance to the Olympic Movement, the NOCs demanded that they receive a greater share of the income generated from Games revenue (especially from television rights) and be given a greater voice in determining Olympic policy. According to Hill (1996), the NOCs complained about the IOC's apparent absolute power, compared to their relative limitations. To address this imbalance some NOCs believed that they should have greater representation on the IOC. A number of these critics went so far as suggesting that every NOC should have a seat on the IOC (Hill, 1996) or a separate organization for the NOCs (Senn, 1999). The first of these propositions was disregarded because of the obvious increase in the size of the IOC that it would have entailed. However, the IOC was not entirely unmindful of the NOC's criticism, and, in response, began to consult them more fully, although, as a buffer to directly increasing their power, members also instituted 'a policy of divide and rule, by recognizing a plethora of organizations through which the interests of the ...NOCs are articulated' (Hill, 1996 p. 72).

One of the groups that were constituted was an organization currently known as the Association of National Olympic Committees (ANOC), but which was originally constituted as GANOC (General Assembly of National Olympic Committees).

The ANOC is currently made up of all the 199 NOCs and is divided into five continental associations (IOC, www.olympics.org):

- Africa- ANOCA (Association of National Olympic Committees of Africa);
- America- PASO (Pan American Sports Organization)
- Asia- OCA (Olympic Council of Asia);
- Europe- EOC (European Olympic Committees);
- Oceania- ONOC (Oceania National Olympic Committees).

The ANOC has a number of specific functions. For example, it makes recommendations to the IOC regarding the use of the funds derived from the sale of television rights and intended for the NOCs through the implementation of the Olympic Solidarity programs. Olympic Solidarity was formed in 1961 to develop sports programs for athletes, coaches and officials in third world countries. It has expanded its brief and income as Olympic television revenue has increased, so that the current quadrennial Olympic Solidarity plan (2001- 2004) has a development and assistance budget totaling US$ 209 484 000. This is 740 % higher than the first four- year plan (1985- 1988) (IOC, www.olympic.org). Through this program, the IOC directs as much as $US 90 000 in annual subsidies to every NOC. It also reimburses NOCs for each athlete they send to the Games. As the larger countries can afford to send larger teams, they accordingly benefit more from this particular allocation (Abrahamson & Wharton, 2000).

Presently, ANOC meets at least once every two years to exchange information and knowledge between the NOCs and also in order to consolidate their role and position within the Olympic Movement. According to Senn (1999), when it was first established, GANOC met with initial antagonism from the IOC leadership. However by the 1970s, ANOC had become an established and accepted part of the Olympic Movement.

Relationship of the host National Olympic Committee to the Olympic Games Organizing Committee

The Olympic Charter (2001) states that the organization of the Olympic Games is entrusted by the International Olympic Committee (IOC) to the National Olympic Committee (NOC) of the country of the host city, as well as to the host city itself. The NOC then forms a separate concern, the Organizing Committee for the Olympic Games (OCOG). However, from the time it is first constituted, the OCOG communicates and negotiates directly with the IOC, from which it receives directions, rather than through the NOC. Although each OCOG varies in its structure, its executive body must include the IOC member or members in the host country; the President and Secretary General of the host country's NOC; and at least one member representing, and designated by, the host city. In addition, it generally includes representatives of the public authorities and other leading national citizens (IOC, www.olympic.org).

From the time of its constitution to its liquidation, the OCOG must comply with the Olympic Charter, the Host City Contract entered into between the IOC, the NOC and the host city, and any instructions that it receives from the IOC Executive Board. For the 2000 Sydney Olympic Games, the President of the Australian Olympic Committee (John Coates), its Secretary General (Perry Crosswhite then Craig McLatchey) and the AOC (and also Australian IOC) board members (Kevan Gosper and Phil Coles) were all board members of the Sydney Organizing Committee for the Olympic Games (SOCOG).

Example of a National Olympic Committee: The Australian Olympic Committee
According to the IOC's Encyclopedia of National Olympic Committees (quoted in Gordon, 1994, p. 24) the first iteration of an NOC in Australia was formed before the celebration of the 1896 Athens Olympic Games.

Preparations to ensure the nation's representation in the Olympic Movement were initiated in 1895 with the formation of a committee of senior sports officials who were to meet prior to each Olympic celebration. The committee later adopted a more authoritative stance under the name of the Australian Olympic Council, the name being replaced by the Australian Olympic Federation in 1914.

However, Gordon (1994, p. 24) disputes this version of authorized history and claims that 'no national (or Australasian) Olympic body existed before 1914'. In that year the Olympic Federation of Australia and New Zealand (OFANZ) was formed. Despite its impressive name the body was less than noteworthy. It 'was born in disharmony and rendered lame by the outbreak of war... New Zealand wanted nothing to do with it. It had a nominal base, Sydney, but no president and its most positive decision was ... to finance the sending of athletes to the 1916 Berlin Olympics: a festival that would not take place' (Gordon, 1994, p. 52).

Because of these obvious failings, the OFANZ only existed until 1920, when Australia's first truly national Olympic organization, the Australian Olympic Council was formed. This body changed its name in 1923 to become the Australian Olympic Federation. It kept this nomenclature until 1990, when both its name and its constitution were altered, the latter quite radically. The NOC changed its designation to become the Australian Olympic Committee (AOC). The most radical reform of the Australian NOC, however, was a change in its power base, so that the AOC was 'a committee of sports rather than ... a federation of state representatives' (Gordon, 1994, p. 390) as it had been in the past. In other words, power to govern the organization now resided in the hands of the Australian national sports governing bodies, rather than state Olympic Councils, as had been the case previously.

Today, the AOC remains an Incorporated Association, whose voting members are the national bodies of sports on the Summer and Winter Olympic programs. Every state and territory still has a State Olympic Council, however their main role is to assist with fund raising and Olympic education through programs such as School Resource Kits, the annual Pierre de Coubertin Awards and state and national Australian Olympic Academies (IOC, www.olympics.org.au).

The AOC is a non-profit organization, and has achieved its aim of being independent of government and government funding (with the exception of contributions by State Governments to the Olympic Team Appeal). The funds required for the AOCs activities are generated primarily through its marketing and fundraising programs (AOC, www.olympics.org.au).

Members of the AOC Executive include its President, two Vice Presidents, two members of the IOC in Australia, the Secretary General of the AOC, the Chairperson and Deputy Chairperson of the Athletes Commission, and seven elected members. The positions of President and Vice President are elected from nominations received from any member of the AOC. The seven other elected members of the Executive are voted in from nominations received from the national bodies of sports on the Olympic program. The Chairperson and Deputy Chairperson of the AOC Athletes Commission are elected by the members of the AOC Athletes Commission. Two IOC Members and the Secretary General are members of the Executive by way of their positions. The Secretary General is appointed by the Executive and is a non-voting ex-officio member. Elections are held at the first Annual General Meeting convened after each Summer Olympic Games (AOC, www.olympics.org.au).

The Role of Women in National Olympic Committees
In 1995, the IOC created a "Women and Sport" working group to advise its Executive Board on strategies to improve access and equity for women in sport. This was as a result of increasing awareness of gender inequities in sport and growing pressure from women's groups for the IOC to be more accountable for and responsive to the lack of opportunities for females in competing, officiating and managing sport,

As one outcome from the Women and Sport working group's suggestions, the IOC has added to its Olympic Charter material to augment the document's rather limited rhetoric of equality. For example, it added the following: "the IOC strongly encourages, by appropriate means, the promotion of women in sport at all levels and in all structures, particularly in the executive bodies of national and international sports organizations with a view to the strict application of the principle of equality of men and women" (IOC, 2001, p. 10).

As another, more pragmatic initiative to increase the number of women occupying leadership and administrative positions within the Olympic Movement, the IOC set specific goals for NOCs (and IFs) in terms of the percentages of their executive members who were to be women. It set an initial objective of having women hold at least 10 per cent of positions within NOCs by December 2000. This quota was not met. In 2002, only 66% of the NOCs have achieved this goal. Failure to achieve even this modest goal makes the IOC's current quota, of at least 20% of the positions in all NOC decision-making structures (in particular the executive and legislative bodies) to be held by women by 31 December 2005, appear even less likely to succeed (IOC, http://www.olympic.org/uk/organisation/missions/women/leaders_uk.asp).
While it is easy to criticize the NOCs for not meeting this target, it is also probably unfair to expect them to do so when the percentage of IOC members who are female also falls well below this quota.

Conclusion

It has been alleged that the IOC is superfluous and that the IFs and the NOCs could manage the operation of the Olympic Movement without it (in Hill, 1996). However, NOCs at present vary greatly in their financial and human resources, from the large and wealthy NOCs, which have more than one IOC member on their board, to small, relatively powerless and financially impoverished NOCs, which have neither IOC members on their governing body, nor even permanent staff to implement policy. Nevertheless, despite these variances, it is undeniable that the NOCs are vital contributors to the Olympic Movement and supply it with many differing services, from providing the teams which compete in the Games to delivering Olympic education programs. Most can only do so with the assistance of Olympic Solidarity funds, which come from the IOC. Taken one step backwards, these funds in turn come from television and marketing revenue, which is originally generated from among the 199 countries in which NOCs are based. So, in many ways, the requests of the NOCs for greater influence in Olympic governance have a strong foundation. Whether or not these wishes will eventuate in the future will be determined, in part, by the continued success of the Olympic Games and the IOC's ongoing ability to generate revenue.

Table 1. List of National Olympic Committees (2002) (Source: IOC).

Albania	Algeria	American Samoa	Andorra
Angola	Antigua and Barbuda	Argentina	Armenia
Aruba	Australia	Austria	Azerbaijan
Bahamas	Bahrain	Bangladesh	Barbados
Belarus	Belgium	Belize	Benin
Bermuda	Bhutan	Bolivia	Bosnia and Herzegovina
Botswana	Brazil	British Virgin Islands	Brunei Darussalam
Bulgaria	Burkina Faso	Burundi	Cambodia
Cameroon	Canada	Cape Verde	Cayman Islands
Central African Republic	Chad	Chile	Chinese Taipei
Colombia	Comoros	Congo	Cook Islands
Costa Rica	Croatia	Cuba	Cyprus
Czech Republic	Democratic People's Republic of Korea	Democratic Republic of the Congo	Denmark
Djibouti	Dominica	Dominican Republic	Ecuador
Egypt	El Salvador	Equatorial Guinea	Eritrea
Estonia	Ethiopia	Federated States of Micronesia	Fiji
Finland	Former Yugoslav Republic of Macedonia	Gabon	Gambia
Georgia	Germany	Ghana	Great Britain
Greece	Grenada	Guam	Guatemala
Guinea	Guinea-Bissau	Guyana	Haiti
Honduras	Hong Kong	Hungary	Iceland
India	Indonesia	Iraq	Ireland
Islamic Republic of Iran	Israel	Italy	Ivory Coast
Jamaica	Japan	Jordan	Kazakhstan
Kenya	Korea	Kuwait	Kyrgyzstan
Lao People's Democratic Republic	Latvia	Lebanon	Lesotho
Liberia	Libyan Arab Jamahiriya	Liechtenstein	Lithuania
Luxembourg	Madagascar	Malawi	Malaysia
Maldives	Mali	Malta	Mauritania
Mauritius	Mexico	Moldova	Monaco
Mongolia	Morocco	Mozambique	Myanmar
Namibia	Nauru	Nepal	Netherlands
Netherlands Antilles	New Zealand	Nicaragua	Niger

Table 1 cont...

Nigeria	Nigeria	Norway	Oman
Pakistan	Palau	Palestine	Panama
Papua New Guinea	Paraguay	People's Republic of China	Peru
Philippines	Poland	Portugal	Puerto Rico
Qatar	Romania	Russian Federation	Rwanda
Saint Kitts and Nevis	Saint Lucia	Saint Vincent and the Grenadines	Samoa
San Marino	Sao Tome and Principe	Saudi Arabia	Senegal
Seychelles	Sierra Leone	Singapore	Slovakia
Slovenia	Solomon Islands	Somalia	South Africa
Spain	Sri Lanka	Sudan	Suriname
Swaziland	Sweden	Switzerland	Syrian Arab Republic
Tajikistan	Thailand	Togo	Tonga
Trinidad and Tobago	Tunisia	Turkey	Turkmenistan
Uganda	Ukraine	United Arab Emirates	United Republic of Tanzania
United States of America	Uruguay	Uzbekistan	Vanuatu
Venezuela	Viet Nam	Virgin Islands	Yemen
Yugoslavia	Zambia	Zimbabwe	

References

Abrahamson, A. & Wharton, D. (2000). *Inside IOC's Books: A Tangled Web of Wealth, Mystery,* Los Angeles Times, http://apse.dallasnews.com/contest/2000/writing/over250.enterprise.first2.asp

Australian Olympic Committee (2002). www.olympics.org.au

Gordon, H. (1994). *Australia and the Olympic Games*, St Lucia, Queensland: University of Queensland Press.

Hill, C. (1996). *Olympic Politics* 2nd ed., Manchester: Manchester University Press

International Olympic Committee (2001). *Olympic Charter*, Lausanne: International Olympic Committee.

International Olympic Committee, (2002), www.olympic.org

Senn, A. (1999). *Power, politics and the Olympic Games*, Champaign, IL: Human Kinetics.

Toohey, K. & Veal, A. (2000). *The Olympic Games: A social science perspective*, Oxon, CABI.

Warning, K. (1980). *A political history of the Modern Summer Olympic Games.* Unpublished Masters thesis, California State University, Long Beach.

COMMUNIST SPORT POLICY: PAST, PRESENT AND FUTURE

Tracy Taylor

Introduction

Sport has played a pivotal role in the propagation of the tenets of communism in many socialist countries. This chapter provides an overview of the various roles and forms of sport policy in communist regimes throughout the twentieth century. In many instances, the state used sport as a functional means through which to initiate social change and instigate ideological reform. Throughout the century, changes in economic and political circumstances impacted on the principles, practices and fundamental goals of communist sport policy, resulting in major directional shifts in policy. Every communist country developed its own approach to sport policy influenced by tradition, culture, ethnic composition, religion, geography, economic and social circumstances. However, in conjunction with the many country specific sporting developments, several shared sport policy doctrines existed and it is these commonalities that provide the focus for this chapter.

In the first few years of existence nearly every newly formed communist regime embarked on a slate of programs aimed at societal transformation and restructure. Sport was used as a means to achieve the ideological goals that had propelled communism into existence. Socialist sport systems were initially focused on reforming sport by severing its links to bourgeois or fascist ideals. This involved breaking with systems and structures that were remnants of the overthrown government and class-based sport participation.

Correspondence to: Tracy Taylor, University of Technology, Sydney, PO Box 222, Lindfield, NSW 2070, Australia, Email: Tracy.Taylor@uts.edu.au

Centrally controlled systems and policies that reorganized sport and physical culture were designed and implemented. The emphasis was on encouraging mass participation and the subjugation of class divides. Sport participation reflected communist ideals, it aimed to facilitate collectivist and non-competitive involvement, assist with harmonious development and good health, and support socialist values.

After a settling in period, the initial drive to only promote sport for all and worker sport was supplemented by centralist policies that supported both mass and elite sport. Having re-established competitive sport, elite athletes and international sporting success were used in propaganda to demonstrate the superiority of communism to the West and to foster diplomatic relations with other countries. During this period there was a concentrated and systematic focus on sport policy that supported and resourced Olympic sports and sports with high international profiles. These policies aimed to ensure medal places for communist athletes and in doing so, maintained an international profile for communism and also fostered nationalist sentiments and patriotism at home. The resulting sport systems produced many world champion athletes and facilitated the communist domination of Olympic Games. Following the collapse of communism, allegations of systematic drug taking and illegal behavior in the pursuit of medals emerged and many sport systems have since been totally dismantled. Contemporary sport policy in both communist and former communist countries has overtly been used to signal a separation from past ethically corrupt practices, with the emphasis shifting away from winning at all costs and unquestioned support of elite talent development.

Today, with the disintegration of many communist regimes across Eastern Europe, the place of sport and its strategic orientation in these countries has significantly changed. Sport policy is undergoing massive revision and reconfiguration. This chapter presents some of the major issues in the shifting sport landscapes of former and current communist regimes within a Western interpretive framework. The following is an overview of key themes. Many country specific historical and analytical accounts of sport policy have been written and readers are advised to consult these resources for more comprehensive details of the sport policy initiatives of specific communist countries.

The Evolution of Communist Sport Policy

Each communist country has espoused and practiced sport policy in a unique manner but these policies have been conjoined by a common doctrine. The Soviet Union (USSR), the People's Republic of China (PRC) and the German Democratic Republic (GDR) were the most prominent proponents of communist sport policy. Smaller and less financially wealthy countries often did not place as high a priority on sports development due to resource constraints. However, under socialist regimes, sport policy exhibited a number of common characteristics. These included strong links with communist ideology and its underpinning principles of sport for all; the construction of a well-resourced 'amateur' sport system; banning of 'professional' sport; central control and support of sport in terms of financial resources, facilities and human resources; determination of sport policy by the state and not by independent sport organizations; collective provision of grassroots sport; emphasis on Olympic sports and development of elite athletes; and use of sport to promote nationalist prestige and international relations.

The participation of communist countries at the 1952 Summer Olympic Games in Helsinki, winning twenty-nine percent of medals, was the beginning of a major incursion into the international sport arena. In each subsequent Olympics until 1980 their medal share grew dramatically. While the USSR led the charge, other countries such as the German Democratic Republic demonstrated strong sporting success. In 1976 the GDR placed second to the USSR in the medal tally and outperformed the United States of America (USA), Cuba, Hungary, Rumania and Poland were also strong contenders in the arena of elite sport competition during the communist halcyon period. Sport policy was also inextricably linked to political goals within these communist countries.

Sport fell under the responsibility of the State in most communist countries. Sport policy was centrally determined and reflected the State's political ideology. The most obvious outcome of this centralized system of control and intervention in sport, at least to the rest of world, was the production of an elite athlete system that nurtured a vast pool of talented youngsters into world-class competitors. This talent identification and development system was supported at every level by education, coaching, training and medical institutions. Sports schools were established in the GDR (1949), China (1955), Russia (1964), and Cuba (1969). Gifted young athletes could train and be educated free of charge in these institutions. It has been estimated that the USSR had some 6,250 schools with over two million participants and 50,000 coaches in 1981 (Riordan, 1986). However, communist sport policy was more than just elite sport development.

During each phase of communism, the development of sport and the achievement of sporting excellence was underpinned by socialism and aligned with the respective changing political priorities. In the early years of communism, worker sport and reformation of sport systems into a collective paradigm were actively pursued. This was accompanied by an overt use of sport as a means to achieve communist world domination and as an anti-capitalist stance.

Sport policy and development then evolved into a more competitive period, where sporting success was equated with nationalist pride and inspiration. International sporting events were also used to maintain contact and relations with other socialist states. Sporting excellence came to signify the recognition and consolidation of socialist ideals, led to the reinforcement of the unity of communist countries and was used in promotion of the communist way of life. The use of sport as a vehicle for transporting communist ideals and values was widespread amongst communist states. Alongside the USSR, Cuba, the GDR, PRC and Romania developed sport policy in support of their political orientation (Sugden, Tomlinson & McCartan, 1990). The way in which sport policies were developed and implemented in the achievement of the above is illustrated through selected country overviews.

THE SOVIET UNION

The Soviet Union communist government's use of sport policy as an arsenal in the class wars and as a tool to promote the socialist state was an initiative that would have consequences not only for other communist countries but also for anti-communist governments around the world. From the post 1917 Revolution period until the 1940s, the Soviet Union led the way in communist sport policy.

In its first years of power, the new regime proclaimed that sport was a political institution and needed to be deployed accordingly. Sport was used as a weapon in the fight against capitalism and the promotion of proletarian rights. Sport policy then shifted focus and was employed in the creation of the USSR as a nation state and, just prior to World War II (WWII), the policy devised was one of collaboration with fascist states (Arnaud & Riordan, 1998). After WWII sport policy centered on building international relations and achieving competitive sporting success on the world stage. The emphasis on elite sport and athlete development continued until 1991 when the USSR was dissolved. A brief overview of the main components of this evolution of sport policy in the Soviet Union is provided below.

In the aftermath of the Revolution, organized elite and bourgeoisie sport was dismantled, as it was seen by the State as the antithesis of the collective notions of socialist ideology. Consequently, competitions such as the Olympic Games were treated with disdain as they represented class distinctions, wealth and privilege within a capitalist economy. Sport was restructured to reflect socialist values and used as a vehicle by which to transport these ideals to the entire population.

The Soviet Union was a member of the International Association of Red Sports and Gymnastics Organizations (RSI). Formed in 1921, this association of eight countries believed that sport should be a means to support the proletarian class struggle. The main aim of the RSI was to promote communist strategy within reformist worker sport organizations.

The establishment of the RSI was more about fostering communist ideals than it was about sport development. Competitions and events were organized between worker sports and bourgeois sports associations to allow for revolutionary propaganda to be spread, and provided forums for Soviet sport to be used in the reinforcement of the proletariat sport movement in capitalist countries. The slogan of the 1924 congress of the RSI in Moscow was 'Every worker athlete must be a soldier of the world revolution' (Arnaud & Riordan, 1998).

In 1925 the Soviet Union officially sanctioned the Supreme Council of Physical Culture as the body responsible for sporting organization of the country. The Council initially focused on the development of sport policy to promote the value of sport in the building of good social and personal hygiene. Physical culture, the improvement of health through exercise, was particularly important in a country that had been ravished by war and that had general poor health and fitness. Activity was used as a counter attack on disease and epidemics and designated as important in developing healthy minds and bodies. Young people engaged in robust physical activities at school and enforced exercise routines were present in state controlled workplaces.

The Soviets developed a unique national system of testing and training in sports. The tests were referred to as 'GTO' Gotov k trudu I oborne, ready for labour and defense. It has been estimated that over seventeen million people were tested between 1931-1960 (Louis & Louis, 1988). GTO tests were held for all levels (please explain what you mean by 'levels' – age? Socioeconomic status? skill level?) and it was integral to the entire Soviet physical education and sport training policy. In 1966 the tests were revised to cover all age groups from 14-60 years in gymnastics, running, jumping, throwing, swimming, skiing, and shooting (except for 14-15 year olds). In 1972 the GTO was again revised and the minimum age was lowered to 10 years. It was to be used for direct military training, and to highlight the importance of sport and fitness.

While increasing levels of physical activity and promoting sport for all were the cornerstones of early communist sport policy, other uses for sport subsequently emerged. In 1928 the First Worker Spartakiad was staged in Moscow, where there were team and individual competitions as well as celebratory ceremonies, demonstration events and cultural dancing and music. Following these games the Soviet Union re-aligned its sport policy to embrace the use of the international sport movement to consolidate and unite sport organizations of socialist states. Sport was able to cut across ethnic, race, religious and cultural differences and therefore was a powerful tool for nationalist agendas. The sport that the Soviets excelled at, football, became its ambassador game. An extensive program of matches between neighboring socialist countries was undertaken to promote better relations and strengthen political ties. Sporting victories and excellence were used as a demonstration of the superiority of the Soviet system. The RSI was dissolved in 1937 and this signaled the USSR's move into international bourgeois sport.

A shift in Soviet sport policy occurred in 1939 when the USSR signed a sports agreement with Germany, facilitating a massive exchange of athletes. Over the next few years, the Soviets engaged extensively in sporting competitions with fascist regimes for political liaison purposes. However, changing political alliances ended this sporting relationship in the early 1940s.

The USSR then began to broaden its sporting horizons to the international arena. In 1947 a special resolution was issued declaring that sporting records would not elicit monetary reward, which they had garnered in the past, but rather the reward would be in medals only. This move, combined with the declaration that proficient athletes would be classified as students or servicemen, qualified Soviet athletes as 'amateur' and able to compete in the Olympics. An allied benefit of developing sport through armed and security forces was the use of vast military resources to train athletes and provide access to costly facilities and equipment. However, the war and associated political upheavals meant that the USSR would have to wait until the 1952 Olympic Games to compete on the world's stage.

Soviet sport associations engaged in a concerted effort to build bridges with international sports federations, engaging in competitions and obtaining affiliation. Their entrée into Olympic Games competition in 1952 was rewarded with 22 gold medals, 30 silver and 19 bronze, a credible performance which grew in stature with each subsequent Games. Sporting success was touted as proof of socialism's superiority; sporting victories enthused national patriotism and triumphs assisted in the preservation of national unity in a country that encompassed a massive diversity of nationalities.

In 1968 the sports system was placed under direct government control with the formation of an All-Union Committee on Physical Culture and Sport. The new committee was to promote physical culture, encourage systematic training on a large scale, raise the standard of sport, prepare competitors for world championships and build sports facilities. While mass participation was a stated goal of the committee, the clear emphasis was on providing a well-resourced system of talent identification and development that produced world-class athletes (Louis & Louis, 1980).

Up until its dissolution, the Soviet Union utilized sport policy to provide a range of sporting opportunities to its population to improve physical and social health. Sport was also used to imbue socialist values such as loyalty, cooperation and discipline, to create social networks in workplaces and urban neighborhoods, and to cultivate competitiveness and success at elite levels. The result was a sport system where sporting participation was encouraged, highly valued and available to all citizens for little cost (Riordan, 1977).

GERMAN DEMOCRATIC REPUBLIC
In the GDR, sport was a cornerstone in the development of a new national identity that was to be distinctive from Nazism and fascism and superior to West Germany. Since sport had enjoyed privileged status under Nazi rule, the new regime proceeded with caution, mindful of how sport clubs had been used to spread fascism. The GDR sport system was similar to the one built in the USSR and provided the basis for international recognition through the sporting successes achieved by its athletes. Sport policy was embedded into an all-encompassing social system and aimed to achieve political and sporting status for the GDR on the world stage.

From modest beginnings after the end of WWII, the GDR quickly developed a pool of athletes who were internationally competitive and provided the GDR with the basis from which to gain membership into the International Olympic Committee. The development of sport was fully supported by trade unions and industries that built new facilities and worked with the Freie Deutsche Jugend (Free German Youth) to promote community sport. In 1952 the State Committee for Physical Culture and Sport (Staatliches Komitee fur Korperkultur und Sport) was established to develop sport policy under the control of the Party's Central Committee. In 1957 the formation of the Deutscher Turn- und Sportbund (DTSB), an executive body with full control of sport planning and finance, signaled a fundamental change in GDR sport, shifting its focus to international competition. The DTSB controlled elite sport, sports boarding schools, sports medicine, and the training of all professional coaches and sports doctors (Naul & Hardman, 2002).

Sport policy concentrated on initiatives that would gain the GDR international membership rights. Determined efforts and a well-resourced political commitment from sporting organizations were instrumental in helping the GDR to obtain international recognition. The GDR hosted events that attracted international competitors and GDR athletes competed in a range of unofficial international events in an attempt to gain official recognition.

The Sport for All programs in the GDR were organized in state institutions and organizations and state-owned firms. The Central Committee set targets for each sport. The school sports systems fed into sports clubs and special training centers, children at sport boarding schools trained up to twenty hours per week at their sport, and adult athletes were also pushed hard. Employers were obliged to release nominated personnel for up to sixteen hours per week for training. Each club operated on a standardized approach to training under the guidance of a staff of coaching and sports medicine specialists (Naul & Hardman, 2002).

West Germany and the GDR had competed as one team in the 1956 and 1960 Olympics. However, in 1972 the GDR competed at the Munich Games as a second German state and brought home medals in gymnastics, swimming and track and field - sports that they had specifically targeted for development. This entrée into the Games and the GDR's success was a culmination of 25 years of intensive sporting and diplomatic activity. The GDR went on to achieve numerous Olympic successes in the 1970s and 1980s. These sporting victories had implications beyond the competition arena, placing the GDR on a world stage and playing a vital role in promoting international relations and providing credibility. The ethical stance and practices employed by the GDR's impressive elite sport system would be called into question after the fall of the Berlin Wall in 1989.

PEOPLE'S REPUBLIC OF CHINA

The precursors of communist sport policy in China were the Red Sports Movement and the New Sports Movement. These two movements had established mass programs of physical exercise for peasants and workers before liberation and the communist party built on these already existing platforms of sport participation. Communist party ideologically was imparted through sport policy by two key bodies after liberation. The All-China Sports Federation (established after Liberation in 1949) was responsible for organized government involvement in sport and the State Sports Commission (established in 1952) provided the guidelines for policy implementation.

Similar to the Soviet Union, the PRC focused its early sport policy on using physical culture to improve the health of its population and to promote socialist goals. In doing so, the PRC moved from the previously established system of voluntary and decentralized sport organizations to a centralized system of sport policy, with sports administration committees established at every provincial and county level. While there has been some variation over time, the essential elements and the centralist control of sport policy within the PRC has remained in place.

The 'Competitive Sports System of the PRC' in 1956 listed competitive level sports, established a National Games, and initiated an athlete-training program under a Ministry directive. Institutes of physical culture, schools and colleges were built for physical culture training. Schools engaged in official exercise programs and exercise breaks were introduced into workplaces in attempts to mobilize the whole population to become physically active. In 1959 the first National Sports Games were held, underpinned by an ethos of unity and collective achievement rather than individual success and glory (Xiangjun & Brownell, 1996). Throughout the 1950s, Chinese sports officials, coaches and athletes were sent to the USSR to learn the latest techniques and to observe the Soviet system in action. Soviet coaches were invited back to China to coach courses. These exchanges had many influences on the PRC sport policies and sport system development. In particular, Soviet female athletes provided strong role models for Chinese women to engage in elite sport. Investment in high level competitive sport was substantial during this period and elite sport was at the centre of sport policy (Jinxia, 2001).

However, this era of intensive concentration on elite sport was quickly followed by a decreased focus on physical culture and a scaling down of the schools and institutes during1960-3 when the economy was in decline. From 1963-66 sport development resumed and greater involvement in international sporting competitions ensued with a concentration on resourcing a limited number of elite athletes.

In a dramatic turn, from 1966-1976, during the Great Cultural Revolution, sport policy was virtually dismantled. It was then slowly resurrected after the overthrow of the Gang of Four. The Cultural Revolution ideals supported sport for the masses and not elite development or sport for the sake of winning medals. In 1968 an order was issued to dismantle the sports ministry and sport commissions in every province and local domain. Several former sports ministry officials were subsequently jailed, beaten and labeled traitors due to their past support of elite athlete development and neglect of mass physical education. Many elite athletes and coaches were also denounced. Sports schools closed, competitions were cancelled and Chinese sports teams ceased to travel outside the country. The slogan of this period was 'friendship first, competition second'.

Athletes were instructed not to hurt each other in the course of play, spectators were to applaud both sides and peasants, workers and soldiers were appointed as sport commentators and called on to judge appropriate athlete behavior (Hong, 1999). From 1971 to 1976, sport re-emerged for political and diplomatic reasons and participation increased at both mass and elite levels. The background and implications of this emergence is discussed further in the section on sport policy and international relations.

The PRCs reinstatement into the International Olympic Committee (IOC), involvement in the Asian Games, bonuses and subsidies for athletes, links with international sports organizations and a heightened involvement of foreign experts in coaching and technical development characterized the new era in sport policy. The policy change involved the adoption of Central Document Number Twenty (1984) which provided guidelines for the development of mass physical culture and led to an increase in corporate sponsorship of sport teams and events and facilitated an increase in the number of sports teams outside the sport commission system. Another key policy initiative was the 1987 approval of 55 institutes of higher education to create elite sport teams, making sport an attractive career option (Xiangjun & Brownell, 1996). The focus on elite athlete development remained in place throughout the 1980s.

OTHER COMMUNIST COUNTRIES
In Cuba, state involvement in sport has been a distinct policy of the revolutionary government. Cuba has used sport for nation building and political socialization whilst achieving mass participation in sport and producing world-class athletes. All sports in Cuba have received state funding since the early 1960s. Professional sport was banned in 1962, entrance charges for sport events were outlawed in 1967, and private clubs were converted to state centers. The National Institute for Sports, Physical Education and Recreation (INDER) was established to determine sport policy, control physical education, sports schools, sports centers, sports teachers and coaches and be responsible for the Cuban national teams. Sport policies generated at the national level were implemented countrywide and strictly centrally controlled. All policies pursued related to the foundation objectives of mass participation and/or developing elite sport.

Sport has featured as a key element in post-revolution Cuban foreign policy. Sport has been used as a mechanism through which to combat political isolation and deal with antagonistic United States (US) policy. The Cubans made a political statement through sport in their boycott of the 1984 and 1988 Olympic Games and have used their involvement in international sporting competitions as a means to diplomatic recognition. As with many other socialist countries, Cuba has promoted the international success of its athletes as an indication of the prowess of its political system. The propaganda sections of sport associations of the socialist bloc convened regular meetings with the aim of using sport to promote the international reputation of socialism. In particular, Cuba focused on building its influence within the rest of Latin America and developing countries, taking on a leadership role and supplying technical expertise, sports aid and training (Pettavion & Pye, 1996).

Hungary operated under a centralized socialist government from 1949-1989 that controlled all aspects of sport policy. There was already a strong tradition of sport involvement in Hungary, with earlier governments supporting sport development, however, central government control intensified under the Hungarian Socialist Workers' Party and sport was increasingly used as a means to engage in foreign and domestic policy goals. The National Office for Physical Education and Sports (NOPES) was the controlling body of all sport in Hungary. Sports clubs and leisure centers were free of charge and the government funded sport facilities. Policy was focused in three areas: school sport; elite sport; and recreation. However, much of the funding and support was directed into elite sport.

As with other communist countries, top echelon Hungarian athletes were put forward as role models and were expected to serve diplomatic functions and be examples of the superiority of the socialist system. Olympic sports or sports which offered good chances of international success were provided with substantial support as these provided the best opportunity to demonstrate the superiority of socialist ideals to the Western world. For ideological reasons, professional sports, foreign athletes, coaches and managers were banned under the socialist regime (Foldesi, 1996).

Bulgaria was another socialist country which built a significant sport system based on socialist sports policies. Just before the political collapse of 1989, they had 585 talent identification and elite athlete development sport centers for children and adolescents and over 1000 school sport divisions that aimed to increase the level of physically active children complemented the elite athlete programs (Girginov, 2001).

Sport policy and international relations
Communist sport policy has reflected the belief that sport can be used to progress countries towards better international relations. There are numerous examples of incidents where sport has been used as a means to promote a healthier relationship between communist and capitalist countries. For example, both Cuban and Hungarian sport policy was used to improve political relations and counter political isolation. In most instances, domestic and foreign policy goals were regarded as complementary.

When the administration of US President Richard Nixon sent a table tennis team to the People's Republic of China (PRC) in 1971, followed by a basketball tour, the occasions reflected a tentative step towards building relationships between the PRC and the USA. These moves were propelled by concern in Beijing that the Soviet Union might escalate its clashes with China and have been referred to as the era of 'Ping-Pong Diplomacy' (Hong, 1999). The PRC excelled at table tennis and the US at basketball, the choice of these sports was diplomatic and designed to ensure no loss of prestige occurred for the host or touring side (Houlihan, 1994). The PRCs use of sport as a means to rebuild international relations also fostered sporting engagements with Japan and Britain. The aim of the PRC sport policy in the 1970s was to gain membership of international sports federations, after its 1958 withdrawal from the IOC over the two China's issue. However, success with the IOC was somewhat complicated due to the recognition of Taiwan as representative of China. During the 1960s when the PRC withdrew from international sporting fixtures, the IOC had granted the China position to Taiwan. Thus, in the 1970s when the PRC returned to the international sporting scene, there was an issue over which identity would be officially recognized.

It was not until 1979 that a compromise was reached which allowed both countries to be individually recognized within the Olympic movement. Please see chapter on National Olympic Committees in this volume.

However, just as sport was used to foster links between countries, it also got caught up in the souring of relationships. Take for example the defection of West German athletes to East Germany in the 1950s and the defection of fifty Hungarians at the 1956 Melbourne Olympics. In each case, the destination country claimed the defections as a political coup.

The defection of Hu Na, an national tennis player, from the PRC to the USA in 1982 generated considerable diplomatic angst at a time when the two countries were locked in negotiations over trade and commerce arrangements (Houlihan, 1994). The defection of Nadia Comaneci, the darling of the 1976 Olympics, received intensive media coverage in the US even though she had retired in 1984. Prior to Nadia's defection, the Romanian government, at the time headed by Nicolas Ceausescu, restricted her movements, fearing that she may defect. In November 1989, she escaped through a hole in the fence, left the country and headed to Austria, where she sought asylum at the US Embassy before moving to the US. The Western media used Comaneci's defection to the West to draw international attention to the brutality of the Ceausescu regime.

Post- WWII Olympic Games are salient indicators of how sport policy and international relations intersect.

- From the 1948 London Games onwards, the power and ideological struggle between the East and West was apparent. Political defections of Czech and Hungarian athletes during the London Games were used for political point scoring.
- The 1952 Games in Helsinki was notable for the re-entry of Russia onto the world sport stage, and the boycott of the PRC.
- At the Melbourne Games in 1956, Russian military action in Hungary led to a political boycott by the Netherlands, Spain and Switzerland, and the PRC withdrew because of the presence of Nationalist China.
- At the Rome Olympics in 1960 the Olympic Village was designed to physically segregate the East and West.
- The Tokyo Games in 1964 saw continued defections from East to West, one from West to East, and the exclusion of North Korean athletes.

- In 1968, Germany was represented by two teams at Mexico City and political activism was potently evident.
- Cold war politics were overshadowed by the 1972 Munich Games massacre, where eleven Israelis, five terrorists and one German policeman were killed.
- The 1976 Games in Montreal strained diplomatic relations between countries and created political turmoil. The Canadian government refused to permit Taiwan to compete after political and economic pressures were applied by the PRC, causing Canada to impose strict terms on Taiwanese participation. The terms were rejected by Taiwan who would only compete as the Republic of China.
- The United States led a boycott of the 1980 Moscow Summer Olympic Games in response to the Soviet invasion of Afghanistan.
- In Los Angeles in 1984 the Soviet Union declined to participate because of lack of compliance with Olympic ideals by the USA.
- The Seoul Games, in 1988, marked the return of the USSR, USA and GDR to head to head competition and were the last Games where the Soviet Union and the GDR competed.

Sport and nationalism

For many communist countries, sport was an expedient vehicle to use in building a unified state. It was believed that sport could transcend differences in education, language, religion and ethnicity and strengthen both mind and body. Sporting success was also an avenue to demonstrate superiority as a country and to celebrate national identity, national vitality and prestige. Sport has also been employed as an unobtrusive form of nationalistic propaganda.

Forging a cohesive national identity was a difficult proposition in many communist countries due to their incredibly diverse ethnic inhabitants. Sport was used to build nationalist sentiments and encourage country specific identification. China's massive population of over a billion people contained more than a dozen ethnic groups, while the USSR featured over 100 nationalities, speaking nearly 100 different languages. Both countries used sport to assist with the integration of these diverse peoples and build nationalist commitments that surpassed all other affiliations (Riordan & Krüger, 1999).

Communist China embraced sport as a means to promote an intense nationalism. This use of sport was particularly evident during international competitions. Through the 1950s, elite sport symbolized national pride. During the Cultural Revolution, sport policy took a dramatic turn, as described in the Sport policy and international relations section above, and sport policy played a major role in the dissemination of political ideals. Sporting fields were extensively used to put principles of a classless society into practice. Millions of Chinese peasants engaged in sports for the first time, women were encouraged into sports in unpredicted numbers, and sport was used to unite urban and country populations. Sport policies were designed to inspire patriotism. After the Cultural Revolution, competitive sport was re-instated and used as a means to demonstrate Chinese progress and foster nationalism through sporting success (Hong, 2001).

Cubans have been encouraged to be involved in building feelings of national honor and identification through sports involvement. The Cuban goal of mass sport participation focused on the development of a cohesive, mutually supportive and classless society. However, this participatory model was not extended to policy decision-making, as all sport policy was developed by the State and Party at the highest levels. In Cuba, champion sportspersons were used as role models for the revolution, and sports successes were used to generate national pride. Cuban athletes have regularly acknowledged the support of the People and the State in victory speeches or dedicated medals to all Cubans. A well known example of athlete subjugation to the state occurred when boxing great Teofilo Stevenson publicly turned down an offer of five million dollars from American promoters to turn professional and fight the then world heavyweight champion Muhammad Ali after the 1976 Montreal Olympics. "What is 5 million dollars against five million Cubans who love me?" asked Stevenson.

In summary, the communist focus on the development of a sports system that systematically produced world champion athletes, coaches and sports related personnel, such as sport scientists, was used to demonstrate socialist supremacy. The level of commitment, from government policy to resources, to the development of elite amateur athletes, was fulsome and unrivalled in Western capitalist countries. The other key feature of communist sport policy was the use of sport for a range of social changes such as improved health, increased labor productivity, and unification of a diverse ethnic population. International recognition and prestige were internally linked to aspects of nationalism and patriotism and externally used in the realm of international relations.

Another salient feature of communist sport policy was the focus on the development of women's sport. The GDR was prominent in its concentration on elite female athletes producing many world champions and successful women's teams. Countries with significant Muslim populations, such as Albania and Afghanistan, deliberately used sport to diffuse prejudges and promote emancipation for women (Riordan & Krüger, 1999). From the earliest years of the PRC, sport policy promoted women's sport and the numbers of female participants, coaches and administers numbers grew. Women were encouraged into national and international competitions as a sign of social and cultural change in the country. During the Cultural Revolution, in a formal program of equality across all social and economic domains, Chinese women were further encouraged into physical activity. After the Revolution, this large participant base was built on for elite sport development, the result was the emergence of very successful Chinese female athletes in gymnastics, diving, badminton, shooting, table tennis and volleyball.

Recent developments in communist sport policy

The collapse of the Soviet empire and the reunification of Germany have significantly re-positioned the place of communist sport policy on the global stage. The collapse of communism has given the Council of Europe a renewed role in regional politics and put it in a good position to use sport to achieve its objectives. The Council of Europe gained the membership of Hungary (1990), Poland (1991), Bulgaria (1992), Estonia, Lithuania, Romania, Slovenia, Slovakia, Czech Republic (1993), Albania (1995), Latvia (1995), Moldova, Ukraine and former Yugoslav Republic of Macedonia (1995), Croatia (1996), the Russian Federation (1996), and Azerbaijan (2001). The Council of Europe promotes sport for all as a means of improving the quality of life, facilitating social integration and contributing to social cohesion, particularly among young people, and fosters tolerance through sport (http://www.coe.int/T/E/Cultural%5FCo-operation/Sport/).

The elite sports systems and associated successes and excesses under communist rule have been turned upside down in many post-communist countries, where sport has been linked to corruption and unethical practices. The priority given to Olympic sports and elite athlete preparation has been called into question, especially in countries which are now struggling with down turned economies and ideological shifts in the use of sport success as an indicator of superiority of political system.

Former GDR sports associations merged with their West German counterparts, and clubs associated with the army or the Ministry of State Security and training centre for elite athletes were closed. The Unification Treaty (1990) called for the restructuring of the three key elite sport developments centers in the former GDR and the entire GDR sports system was dismantled in the 1990s. The whole question of the use of state-sponsored doping of athletes in the GDR have cast a taint on previous sporting victories of athletes from communist countries.

In 1999 the former head of sport in East Germany and a leading sports doctor were charged for their alleged roles in setting up a state-run doping system in the 1970s and 80s. They were indicted after investigations into revelations of a state-run systematic doping policy and were charged with being an accessory to causing bodily harm to 142 young female swimmers and athletes through the administration of banned substances. Nine doctors and coaches were also fined, and over 500 people suspected of being involved, including senior government officials who had given approval to the policy, were investigated.

Communist countries

Since 1991 the face of Russian sport has taken on a new look. This change in sport policy has involved the reorganization of sports administration, decreases in financial subsidies for Soviet state committees, introduction of a self-supporting accounting system and democratization of the state controlled system for sports. Sporting exchanges with Western societies and the introduction of new sports such as American football and oriental military arts like karate have occurred. In a dramatic shift, sports officials have given permission, and even encouraged, athletes to play abroad in professional teams. These initiatives suggest that the new socialist sports system will unite both the socialist state sports systems and democratic sports systems.

Russian sports teams have continued to perform well despite the huge decrease in financial support. Their Olympic team finished second to the United States in the medal tally at the 2000 Summer Olympics in Sydney, and third behind Germany and Norway at the last Winter Olympics in Nagano, 1998. Russia is no longer considered the sporting powerhouse it once was and many Russian athletes are engaged in professional sports outside of the country. As government resources decline, Russian sport will need to gain private and corporate sponsorship to remain internationally competitive.

In Cuba the state control of sport will no doubt be under increasing pressure from global trends in professionalization, sport commercialism and business.   The financial resources committed to sport development, particularly at the elite athlete level, may also come under question in the future.   The use of sport as socialist propaganda has also weakened.   The argument that sporting prowess demonstrates a superior social system is no longer valid in the face of the collapse of many former communist allied countries.   It is likely that Cuba will continue to be committed to promoting socialist internationalism through sport policy but the reduction in economic support from the former Soviet Union and Eastern Europe will have an impact on the level to which this will be possible.

Chinese sport policy continues to facilitate both mass participation in sport and development of elite athletes, coaches and support personnel. However, in a significant change, China reformed its national sports system in 1993 and began a program of promoting commercial development in sport.   This move signaled a shift from a totally state funded sport system to one that encouraged sport as business (Hong, 2001).

Post-communist countries
With the decline of communism as a world force during the 1980s, the accompanying unifying ideology dissipated, so national and religious identities began to reassert their power in many post-communist countries. Many of the former communist countries faced a significant transitional crisis.   Former comrades and allies became competitors or enemies, and former enemies became allies.   Words, meaning, actions, values, symbols, myths, expectations and roles of sport within these changed communities are undergoing massive adaptation.

In the new Federal Republic of Germany (FDR), sports clubs and federation are autonomous units funded by the government under the responsibility of one of the seventeen laender (federal states) of which six are 'new' laender admitted after the dissolution of the GDR.   The collapse of the GDR meant the end of centrally controlled sports and the establishment of new sports federations, association and clubs within these areas.   Competitive sports and Sport for All are under the control of the German Sports Federation (DSB) and its member organizations.

The federal government is responsible for sport policy that is of central importance to the FDR. It represents the entire nation in sport, represents the state at events such as the Olympic Games, and develops international sports policies including foreign relations through sport development in Third World countries. As a reaction against the experiences of sport used by the Third Reich as a political platform sport policy, in the FDR there is strict division between the voluntary, non-profit sports organizations and the state (Heinemann, 1996).

Hungary's sport system has also been massively restructured post-1989 with a lessening of government control, regulatory policies and funding. Many sport organizations divested themselves of government control and a new national sports authority manages and co-ordinates sport policy. Former sports organizations have been converted into voluntary organization, however, the focus of Hungary's sport policy is still the national importance of sport and physical education. Recent sport policy has moved to differentiate itself from its links with developing and promoting communist ideals, and away from use in international relations to more of a domestic nationalism role.

Corporate and private funding of sport has started to emerge and sports such as aerobics, which are non-Olympic, have begun to attract increasing numbers of participants in post-socialist Hungary. The former socialist government's sport policy required subsidized ticket prices at sports events, which has been gradually withdrawn and user pay systems introduced for sport courses, however a degree of central subsidy has remained. Priority has been given to development of sports clubs, and with this, elite sport development via the clubs. Numbers of foreign athletes have increased since the lifting of the ban on their participation in Hungarian sport teams. The influx of foreign athletes and coaches has mainly been from former socialist countries.

Sport policy is in a transitional stage in Hungary and has yet to establish a clear long-term vision for sport. Given this, and its recent economic and political problems, the future of sport in Hungary is difficult to predict (Foldesi, 1996).

Sport in Bulgaria was also affected by the transition between the socialist regime and the new government and its policies. The Committee for Youth Physical Education and Sport (CYPES) was formed in 1992 to dismantle the Bulgarian Sports Union (this was completed in 1998) and set national sport policy. The latter was accomplished by moving Bulgaria to a sport system that was divested of central government control. CYPES was renamed the State Agency for Youth and Sport in 2000 and is the body that sets national sport policy. While sport for all and competitive sport are still major tenets of the country's sport policy, it has been suggested that in its quest for Europeanization, sport policy has concentrated its efforts on the national and international development of elite sports to the detriment of sport policy making at the grass roots level (Girginov, 2001).

In some countries, the transition from the old world of communist sport to the new post-communist world has taken on unexpected political debates. In Croatia, football has been used to both gain international legitimacy and to symbolize the move away from communism. In the first instance it has been argued that the newly established Croatian government, headed by Franjo Tudjman, used the 1990 US-Croatian football match as a public relations exercise. The symbolism of this match was to convey the message that Croatia was informally being recognized by the US as an independent state, despite the fact that at the time of the game the Yugoslav Federation still existed. The match provided a forum for Croatia to enhance its image on the sporting stage of the world. Thus, football was used to further political interests in building national unity and mobilizing support for the inevitable civil war that was to come (see Sack & Suster, 2000 for a more detailed analysis). However, in an ironic twist, Tudjman's subsequent use of football in the political arena would lead to his alienation from many traditional football supporters. The battle over this post-communism control of the sport was about the politically imposed name change of the Zagreb Premier League Football Club from 'Dinamo' to 'Croatia'. According to President Tudjman, 'Dynamo' had a particular meaning in official communist vocabulary, as well as a symbolic function in the communist organization of sport, a meaning which did not represent the post-communist commitment to a more national Croatia   (Vrcan, 2002). Therefore, the Croatian nationalist movement viewed a name change as necessary to symbolize a break with the past and the engagement with the new nationalist Croatia.

On the other side, the club's core group of fans, the Bad Blue Boys (BBB) opposed a name change, feeling that the meaning of 'dynamo' was beyond the political and represented their collective identity as committed football fans. For his efforts, Franjo Tuđman, the first president of the independent Croatian state, was welcomed at Maksimir stadium in 1996 with an uproar of disapproval and abuses, the entire stadium was adorned with banners reading "DINAMO" and placards with that read: 'Had there been freedom and democracy, it would have been Dinamo and not Croatia'. Soon after his death in 1999 the club's name was changed to Dinamo Zagreb. It is interesting to note that in this example, sport is still being used as a political tool and to promote a certain notion of nation-state.

The Future
The emergence of a global sporting spectrum and the shift from amateur to professional sport has created a very different sporting world today. The international sporting community has embraced sport as business - a truly westernized conceptualization of sport. Sport has endured as a vehicle for nationalism, pride and patriotism. States emerging from the collapse of communism have sought international recognition through sporting competitions, membership of internal sport federation and recognition by the IOC.

While the former Soviet Union used sport policy to develop as a form of international relations and to demonstrate its strength to the world, the state funds associated with such a wholesale initiative were huge and not sustainable after the collapse of the Soviet empire. Incongruently, the claim that sporting success was related to the superiority of the communist socio-economic system could no longer be maintained when the system fell apart amidst continued athletic triumphs. Communist sport policy is now primarily represented by China, Cuba and North Korea.

The value of being a host of the Olympic Games is still seen paramount by many countries. China's desire to host the Olympic Games ranged over several bids, costing millions of dollars, and they finally succeeded with the award of the 2008 Games to Beijing. Bidding for the Olympics was used to fuel nationalist fervor with slogans such as "A more open China awaits the 2000 Olympic Games," and "An honor for Beijing, a chance for China." The awarding of the Games to China was a controversial decision due to the poor track record of the Chinese on human rights. The IOC contended that China will use the preparation period before the times as an opportunity to address human rights issues, while cynics claim the Chinese are using the Games as an element in a broader and more comprehensive political strategy. The use of the Olympics for political point scoring continues unabated.

In Cuba, past sporting success was an outcome of a significant financial commitment and support from wealthy communist countries. However, the resources that were dedicated to creating widespread physical culture development and elite athlete support may now be under increasing scrutiny as the gap widens between grass root participation and top athletes and pressures emerge for the financial resources required to operate such an intensive sport system to be redirected into other areas such as health and housing.

The decrease in government funding has opened sport systems up to market forces and private sport clubs and commercialized sport. The reduction in resources supplied by former powerful communist states, and declining sport related support has significantly impacted on the less well-resourced communist countries. The use of success in sport to gain international prestige, to signal an effective and pervasive social system, to showcase nationalism, unite diverse ethnic groups, and to promote socialist ideals has been further significantly impacted by the communist crisis. These political changes have de-stabilized sport and caused government to rethink their sport polices and priorities.

Each communist regime has its own distinctive blend of history, culture, economics, and social interactions that, at the end of the day, produced unique country-specific sport policies. As political agendas have changed, fundamental communist principles that underpinned sport policies for most of the twentieth century are no longer relevant for many countries. Globalization and commercialization pressures that have impinged on sports worldwide, will also impact communist sport in the twenty-first century. Sport policy is in a period of transition in communist countries and the new place and role of sport within these regimes is not yet fully apparent.

References

Chalip, L., Johnson, A. & Stachura, L. (1996). (Eds) *National Sports Policies: An international handbook*. Westport: Greenwood Press.

Foldesi, G. (1996). Sport policy in Hungary. In Chalip, L., Johnson, A., & Stachura, L. (Eds) *National Sports Policies: An international handbook*. Westport: Greenwood Press, 187-211.

Girginov, V. (2001). Strategic relations and sport policy making: The case of aerobic union and school sports federation Bulgaria. *Journal of sport management* 15(3), July 2001, 173-194

Jones, R. & Riordan, J. (1999). Sport and Physical Education in China.

Hong, F.(1999) Not all bad! Communism, society and sport in the Great Proletarian Cultural Revolution: a revisionist perspective. *International journal of the history of sport,* 16(3), 47-71.

Hong, F.(2001) Two roads to China: The inadequate and the adequate. *International journal of the history of sport,* 18(2), 148-167.

Houlihan, B. (1994) *Sport and international politics: a comparative analysis*. Hemel Hempstead: Harvester Wheatsheaf.

Houlihan, B. (1996). *Sport, policy and politics: a comparative analysis;* Routledge.

Jinxia, D. (2001). The female dragons awake: women, sport and society in the early years of the new China. *International journal of the history of sport* 18(2), 1-34

Louis, V. & Louis, J. (1980). *Sport in the Soviet Union*. (2nd Ed) Oxford: Pergamon Press.

Naul, R. & Hardman, K. (2002). (Eds) *Sport and Physical Education in Germany*. London: Routledge.

Pettavanio, P. & Pye, G. (1996). Sport in Cuba. In L. Chalip, A. Johnson & L. Stachura (Eds) *National Sports Policies*: *An international handbook*. Westport: Greenwood Press, 116-139.

Riordan, J. (1977) *Sport in Soviet Society: Development of sport and physical education in Russia and the USSR*. London: Cambridge University Press.

Riordan, J. (1986) Elite sport policy in ease and west. In L. Allsion (Ed.) *The Politics of Sport*. Manchester: Manchester University Press, 66-89.

Riordan, J. (1996). Communist sport policy: The end of a era. In L. Chalip, A. Johnson & L. Stachura (Eds) *National Sports Policies*: *An international handbook*. Westport: Greenwood Press, 89-115.

Riordan, J. & Krüger, A. (1998). *Sport & International Politics*. London: E & FN Spon.

Riordan, J. & Krüger, A. (1999). (Eds) The *International politics of sport in the twentieth century* London: Spon.

Sack, A. & Suster, Z. (2000). Soccer and Croatian nationalism. *International review for the sociology of sport,* 24(3), 305-320.

Sugden, J., Tomlinson, A. & McCartan, E. (1990). The making of while lightening in Cuba: politics, sport and physical educations 30 years after the revolution. *Area Review*, 14 (1) 101-109.

Vrcan, S. (2002). The curious drama of the president of a republic versus a football fan tribe. A symptomatic case in the post-communist transition in Croatia. *International review for the sociology of sport* 37(1), 59-77 http://www.coe.int/T/E/Cultural%5FCo-operation/Sport/, accessed on 2 January 2003.

Xiangjun, C. & Brownell, S. (1996). The People's Republic of China. In L. Chalip, A. Johnson & L. Stachura (Eds) *National Sports Policies*: *An international handbook*. Westport: Greenwood Press, 67-88.

THE 1980 AND 1984 OLYMPIC GAMES BOYCOTTS

Kristine Toohey

Introduction

Politics and the Olympic Games are not unfamiliar companions. Despite denials to the contrary from politicians and Olympic officials, they have been linked to one another in the Olympic arenas, in a multiplicity of overt and also covert ways, since the time of the Ancient Games (Toohey & Veal, 2000). However, in recent years, with the increasing global television reach of the Olympic Movement, there has been an increase in the lure of and return from political capital that the Games can produce. This has turned them into the more vulnerable partner in the relationship.

The political intrusions into the Olympic movement have taken many different forms and involve a number of different entities. For example, the World Wars prevented the celebration of the Games in 1916, 1940 and 1944. But these are by no means the only examples; at all other times, since the IOC was formed in 1894, political machinations have impacted on the Games. Some obvious examples include: the violent suppression of Olympic dissenters by the Mexican government and the political statements of black-power salutes by US athletes at the 1968 Mexico City Olympics; the Palestinian terrorist murder of Israeli athletes at the Munich Olympics of 1972; and the 1976 boycott of the Montreal Games by many African countries in protest against a tour of South Africa by a New Zealand Rugby team.

Correspondence to: Professor Kristine Toohey, Department of Tourism, Leisure, Hotel and Sport Management, Griffith University, PMB 50, Gold Coast Mail Centre, Qld. 9726, Australia

One of the most potent of the political intrusions into the Games has been the use or threat of boycott by national governments. Yet, the International Olympic Committee (IOC), somewhat idealistically, or some would argue hypocritically, has tried to distance itself from the association of sport and politics.   For example, when the IOC Charter (2001, p.15), outlines amongst other things, rules governing participation at an Olympic Games, it states: 'The Olympic Games are competitions between athletes in individual or team events and not between countries. They bring together the athletes designated   for   such   purposes   by   their   respective   NOCs   (IOC, http://multimedia.olympic.org/pdf/en_report_122.pdf).

The inability of the Olympic Family to enforce this assertion, especially in relation to boycotts in the1970s and 80s, demonstrated the strength of the world's political leaders in influencing the celebration of the Games, relative to the limited power of the International Olympic Committee to avoid their interventions.

This chapter examines the two most significant Olympic boycotts, those of 1980 and 1984 and examines how politicians forced their views on their relative National Olympic Committees (NOCs). It is important to note that, in both cases, the government initiating the political action did not use the term 'boycott', but rather 'non-acceptance' for 1980 and 'non-participation' for 1984 (Hill, 1996). Despite such semantic smoke and mirrors, designed to avoid IOC sanctions, they were in fact 'boycotts'. This chapter will refer to them as such.

The 1980 Moscow Olympic Games

In December 1979 the Soviet Union invaded Afghanistan. This military action affected the Olympic movement, primarily through a United States led campaign, for nations not to compete in the 1980 Moscow Olympic Games. In fact, one of the first international diplomatic consequences of the invasion, occurred in January 1980, when the President of the United States, Jimmy Carter, warned that in retaliation for the Soviet action, the United States would withdraw from the Moscow Summer Olympic Games, due to begin in July of that year. Carter initially asked the IOC to move the Games, preferably to Greece. US Congress supported the change of venue, but the IOC rejected his request, as technically the Games are awarded to a city and not a country. In response to the IOC, in February 1980, Carter, now somewhat more knowledgeable about the IOC's Charter, informed the United States Olympic Committee (USOC) that he expected it to withdraw from the Games (Hill, 1999).

After President Carter's initial announcement three main international politically aligned Olympic factions quickly developed; those governments in favor of boycotting the Games, those in favor of competing and those who were, at that point, undecided. Initially, this last group included a number of close US allies. However, during the early part of 1980, the United States strongly lobbied friendly foreign democratic political leaders and consequently international support for Carter's cause slowly increased. Some governments that were in favor of the boycott in turn placed pressure on their NOC and some individual athletes not to attend the Games. The final outcomes of these pressures varied. One example of a country that was initially undecided, but later followed Carter's lead, with all the accompanying national political machinations that followed such a decision was Australia.

Carter's call for the Games to be taken away from Moscow was not the first such appeal. As early as 1978, in the Australian Federal Parliament, Michael Hodgeman, the Liberal Member for Denison, had called for the Games to be withdrawn from Moscow and awarded to an alternative venue. He informed the House of Representatives that in the United Kingdom an all-party Parliamentary Committee was promoting the same objectives, and that in the United States, 35 Senators had publicly expressed a similar opinion. The Liberal Party leader and Prime Minister, Malcolm Fraser, did not support Hodgeman's motion at this juncture and on 10 February 1979, he announced that the federal government would grant $A800 000 to the Australian Olympic Federation (AOF) as support for Australia's participation in the Moscow Olympics. This was the same amount that the government had provided four years earlier for the Australian Olympic team's Montreal preparations. Of this amount, $A100 000 was provided from the 1978-79 Budget and was to be used for pre-training purposes. The balance of $A 700 000 was allocated from the 1979-1980 Budget and this funding was to be used to subsidize expenses incurred by the team at the Olympics (Australia, Parliament, Debates (Representatives), 1978, Vol. H. of R. 111; Australia, Department of Home Affairs, 1979-80 Annual Report).

The Australian Olympic Federation (AOF) welcomed the grant and effusively praised the Federal government. In its 1979-80 Annual Report, (p.7) its Honorary Secretary-General, Julius Patching, wrote; "never in its history, has this Federation received such generous and beneficial support as has been provided to us by our government during this Olympiad".

This harmony was not to continue. In Australia there had been initial hesitation to the proposed US boycott. Prime Minister Fraser stated: "the Games, however, are an international event, not a Russian event, and should be seen in that context" (Fraser, 1980, p. 1). The Minister for Foreign Affairs, Andrew Peacock, reinforced this opinion by reiterating his party's philosophy of non-intervention in sport and claiming that participation in the Games was a matter for the sporting parties concerned. In spite of this rhetoric there was a double standard operating, for, this view was in marked contrast to the government's existing policy of banning Australia's sporting ties with South Africa (Australia, Parliament, Debates (Representatives), 1980, Vol. H. of R. 111).

However, the government's attitude of non-involvement in the Moscow Games was relatively short lived. The Australian government, bowing to US pressure, decided to follow Carter's lead and called upon the AOF to withdraw Australia's team, however not all of its Executive favored such a course of action. Instead of complying with the government's wishes the AOF adopted the position that boycotts had not proven to be effective at past Olympics, since most of the boycotting nations lacked the quantity or quality of competitors to make an impact on the Games' success. Further, the organization, which according to the Olympic Charter, was to have the ultimate decision regarding participation, cautioned that if it followed the Federal government's appeal the current boycott of Moscow could also be a futile gesture (Australia Olympic Federation, 1980). The ongoing disagreement:

> 'amounted to a classic collision between the interests of sport and those of politics, and, because it was portrayed at the time as an issue of huge significance to the security of the nation and to world peace, it forced some agonizing choices between loyalties. It was a traumatic and utterly divisive episode, one that wrecked careers and provoked animosities that endured long after their cause had been buried in old newspaper files'
>
> (Gordon, 1994, p. 323).

The federal Opposition, the Australian Labor Party (ALP), initially agreed to support an effective boycott, that is, one which would be upheld by the major sporting nations of the world. However, when many countries appeared to be reluctant to follow America's lead, the Opposition withdrew its support. The Opposition leader, Bill Hayden, remarked that the government's action of supporting the boycott affected the Kremlin with the power generated by 'the exploding force of a blanc-mange' (Australia, Parliament, Debates (Representatives), 1980, 19 February, Vol. H. of R. 111, p.131). The Opposition did not let the matter rest there. It mounted an attack on the government, accusing it of harassing the AOF and pressuring the major Olympic team sponsors to withdraw their support.

As an example of the pressure applied by the government, the Minister for Home Affairs, Bob Ellicott, threatened to withdraw the athletes' passports, however he swiftly reversed this decision. Although not prepared to ban Australian sportsmen and women from leaving the country, the government showed no reluctance in attempting to influence the AOFs decision and applied restrictions on the utilization of the government's contribution to the Olympic team fund. For example, the grant was not to be used to fund the team's expenses if the Games were held in Moscow; rather the money was to be used expressly for the purpose of subsidizing those athletes who represented Australia at an alternative sports competition (Australia Olympic Federation, 1980).

In addition to the proposed Olympic boycott, the government introduced other sanctions against the Soviet Union. Scientific and cultural exchanges ceased, and fishery agreements were also cancelled. No bans were placed on the export of Australian primary products, such as wool, wheat and rutile. The government rationalized this decision on the grounds that such trade sanctions would be ineffective since the Soviet government could readily obtain these products from other nations. It argued that in the long run, Australians would be the losers. The public could be excused for crediting this decision to more personal motives, when it was revealed that wool purchased from the Prime Minister's property at Nareen was destined for the Soviet market (Cohen, 1980).

In February 1980, the government, acknowledging public sentiment, repeated President Carter's earlier appeal that the Games should still be celebrated, but at a site outside the USSR. Showing a Carter-like ignorance of the reality of the Olympic movement and an idealistic and hypocritical understanding of his own intervention, Prime Minister Fraser talked about a return to the days of 'purism' for the Olympic Games:

'The government places a great deal of importance on being able for the future to re-establish the Olympic ideal in a way which will enable the athletes of the world to compete free of partisan politics of one kind or another. The government has discussed the concept of having a permanent site for the Games in Greece. If that were the wish of a number of governments whose countries are represented on the International Olympic Federation [sic], this government would support not only morally, but also financially, the establishment of that permanent dedicated site under the hands of the Olympic Federation' (Australia, Parliament, Debates (Representatives) Vol. H. of R. 117, 20 February 1980, pp. 97-98).

At its annual conference, on the 19th April 1980, the AOF discussed its official position with regard to participation in the Moscow Olympics. Most of the national sporting organizations were in favor of competing, although the Australian Yachting Federation announced that it would not send a team. Gallup Polls, which had indicated in January that the majority of Australians were in favor of the boycott, had by now registered a shift in public opinion; 55 per cent of those interviewed were now opposed to the government's stance. At the AOF meeting, Bob Ellicott (the Minister for Home Affairs), Andrew Peacock (the Minister for Foreign Affairs), Doug Anthony (the Deputy Prime Minister) and Bill Hayden (the Leader of the Opposition), addressed the Executive Council of the Federation. Anthony then met with all the AOF delegates, but the outcome hoped for by the government was not forthcoming; indeed no decision was taken. Instead, the AOF voted to defer its decision. Finally, in May, the AOF ceased its temporizing and announced it would send a representative Australian team to the Games, with the provision that the Olympic Committees for each sport could make individual decisions on their sport's participation (Cohen, 1980).

The final voting of the AOF had been close—six for and five against the boycott. The President of the AOF, Syd Grange, clarified the decision: "We looked at the attitude of the government; we looked at our responsibility and we tried to reconcile the two and we decided to go" (Lester, 1984,p.206).

The Prime Minister asked the AOF to reconsider its decision, and it agreed to do so. But after further discussions its decision stood, prompting Fraser to observe that its action was "a failure of executive leadership and a denial of national responsibility. Those who have voted to go to Moscow have plainly placed the Olympic movement above Australia's national interest and above the interest of every individual Australian" (Lester, 1984,p.206).

In addition to yachting (which had previously decided to boycott the Games), the boxing, volleyball, equestrian, shooting, and hockey (men's and women's) national federations withdrew. A number of individual athletes also chose to join the boycott. Following this development Bob Ellicott stated that the individual athletes and groups who had agreed to the boycott would receive financial assistance from the Federal government in order to compete in alternative competitions. The national sporting organizations that continued to insist on their prerogative to attend Moscow received a letter of appeal from Ellicott urging them to reconsider their position (Australia, Report to the House of Representatives Standing Committee on Expenditure, 1984).

The federal government then sought approval from the Minister for Finance for a $A 500 000 appropriation to assist Australian athletes and teams to compete in alternative competitions. This approval was granted in July, and the seven relevant national organizations, which had agreed not to compete, shared the sum of $AUS 488 734. However, the proposed alternative Olympic Games did not eventuate. Some competitions in specific sports were held, but not on the scale envisaged by President Carter or Malcolm Fraser (Australia, Report to the House of Representatives Standing Committee on Expenditure, 1984).

Of the original contingent of 270, an Australian team of 190 athletes and officials left for Moscow. In terms of the medal tally, the team bettered Australia's previous effort at Montreal, gaining two gold, two silver, and four bronze medals. A long term result of the pressure placed on the AOF by the Australian government was a policy shift by the AOF to eliminate its dependence on government finance and to seek its funding from the private sector.

A non-Olympic, but another long-term outcome occurred as a direct result of the government's wish for a boycott of the Moscow Olympics. In January 1980, the Australian Institute of Sport (A.I.S.) was founded. Because of the timing of its establishment, in the midst of the anti-Olympic campaign, it has been suggested that this move could be considered to be a direct bribe to elite athletes as the cash payments offered to induce Olympic non-participation (Australia, Parliament, Debates (Representatives), 1980, Vol. H. of R. 119).

Within the US, the interference of politicians in Olympic matters had been similar to that of Australia, however with a different outcome. Carter had bipartisan support for his stance and enormous pressure was placed on the United States Olympic Committee (USOC) from the Democrat and Republican parties alike, both Houses of Congress, and the White House machinery to comply with his requests. Like its Australian counterpart, the USOC initially argued against withdrawing. It suggested that if 'the Games are to be disrupted every time there are human rights violations or aggressions in the world, the Games never would have been conducted for the last twenty-five or thirty years, but this cut no ice' (Hill, 1999, p19).

Carter obviously held a different viewpoint to that of the USOC and insisted that the proposed boycott was intended to defend human rights, international law and the security of not only the US but many other free world nations. He also argued that this action was not in conflict with the United States' commitment to the ideals of Olympic movement. In a somewhat disingenuous vein he also maintained that US sports should still be managed by private organizations and not by the government. Despite such obvious contradictions in his line of reasoning, his political pressure triumphed.

At the decisive USOC meeting, addressed by Vice-President Walter Mondale, those in favor of the boycott won by the relatively easy margin of 1,604 to 797 votes (Hill, 1999).

The Soviets did not accept that their invasion of Afghanistan was the motive for the political intervention and boycott of the Moscow Games. Instead they countered with a proposition that the underlying reasons for the US led campaign were: that the USSR was a socialist country; that President Carter wished to undermine détente; and that he needed to salvage his failing popularity as President. Their campaign's main arguments appeared in _Sovietski Sport_ on January 20th, 1980 (quoted in Hill, 1999, p20):

> "We understand clearly why all real friends of sports and Olympism decisively oppose the provocative maneuvers of supporters of Cold War in the United Sates, England and some other imperialist states, who are striving to utilize sport as an instrument of their policy and hinder the forthcoming meeting of world youth on the arenas of the Moscow Olympic Games... The foreign policy of the USSR which is clear to the peoples of the world, corresponds with their basic interests... and serves as a reliable support of all forces struggling for peace and detente. Supporting the cause of preserving the unity of the Olympic movement, striving to prevent interference of politicians in sport and participating in Moscow's holiday of youth - despite threats, slanderous tricks and political pressure - this is the attitude of the sports world and the public of the countries participating in the Olympic movement toward the Olympiade in the first country of socialism."

Most Western European governments were not as willing as the US or Australia to bring pressure to bear upon their NOCs. The most powerful politicians to follow the American lead were the leaders of West Germany, Japan and Great Britain. However, like its Australian counterpart, the British Olympic Association decided to defy its government and Prime Minister, Margaret Thatcher, and send a team to Moscow. Ultimately, 81 National Olympic Committees participated in the 1980 Summer Olympic Games, compared with 88 at Montreal in 1976, 122 at Munich in1972 and 113 at Mexico City in1968.

In his memoirs, Carter defended his stand and commented that the campaign was more difficult than he had initially envisaged. He believed that the reason for this was that NOCs, for the most part, were independent bodies, whose members deeply resented government involvement in their governance (Hill, 1999). Yet, many accepted government funding. This financial dependence meant that when NOCs failed to comply with their government's requests they faced the threat or possibility of future funding cuts, increased government control and involvement, or having to source alternative sources of funding which would make them less dependent on politicians using them to advance their agendas. For some NOCs, such as the AOF, this was a possibility. For smaller NOCs, especially those from countries with more totalitarian regimes, this model of governance has still not occurred.

1984 Los Angeles Olympic Games

The city of Los Angeles had no serious opposition when it presented its bid to host the 1984 Summer Games, due largely to other cities' fear of repeating the financial disaster of the 1976 Montreal Olympic Games or the terrorist events of the 1972 Munich Games. Due to this, its bid committee was able to 'negotiate an unprecedented contract with the IOC: the local organizing committee and the USOC, not the city, assumed all financial responsibility for hosting the Games' (Andranovich, Burbank & Heying, 2001, p.113), as well as unprecedented independence from government to organize the Games.

Although the USSR did not announce its intention not to compete at the 1984 Games until 8 May, 1984, shortly before the deadline for acceptance of invitations, there had been grave doubts about whether its team would attend ever since the US led campaign to boycott the 1980 Moscow Games. Further political incidents had since added tension to the relationship between the US and the USSR. For example, the Soviet air force shooting down a Korean airliner over Kamchatka, in the far North East of the USSR, in August 1983, had provoked hostile responses throughout the US. As a result of this, the California State Legislature passed a resolution condemning the USSR and recommended that its athletes be banned competing at the 1984 Games.

Another outcome of the Kamchatka incident was the establishment of the 'Ban the Soviets Coalition'. These and other consequences provided the Soviets with some evidence of potential hostility, which could be directed to their athletes and thus provided a justification for Eastern Bloc non-participation (Hill, 1999). Other reasons put forward for their no show were the poor relations between the administrations of US President Reagan and USSR President Chernaenko, and that the Soviets believed that their team would not have performed as well as their American rivals (Reich, 1986).

The Soviets claimed the above suggestions for their non participation were incorrect and that there had been four main issues that had led to their decision: the high cost of the athletes' accommodation in the Olympic Village; the United States government's recognition of Olympic identity cards instead of visas; lack of permission for Aeroflot Airlines to transport Soviet athletes to Los Angeles; and a similar veto of a request for a Soviet ship to dock in Los Angeles harbor. In addition, the US State Department initially refused a visa for the USSR Olympic attaché, claiming that he was a Russian Intelligence Agency KGB official. Interestingly, according to Hill (1999), the USSR criticism was directed towards the US government, rather than the Los Angeles Olympic Organizing Committee (LAOOC).

To counteract the politicians' maneuvers, Peter Ueberroth, President of the LAOOC, lobbied hard to convince the Eastern bloc to compete, however all of the Eastern bloc, with the exception of Romania, followed the USSR lead (Hill, 1999). The Romanians viewed the Olympics as a good opportunity to show the world it could act independently of the USSR. Other socialist countries that were approached by the LAOOC included The Peoples' Republic of China, which competed after a 32-year Olympic Games absence, and East Germany and Cuba, which did not attend. In all, 140 NOCs sent teams, while 17 NOCs did not compete. This number of competing NOCs was inflated by allowing some territories to participate, even though they did not meet Olympic Charter requirements (Hill,1999; Vinokur, http://www.mtholyoke.edu/~skcurtis/alaone.html).

Following the Games, organizers were left with a tangible $US 222.7 million surplus, nearly 40 per cent of which stayed in the Los Angeles area to support youth sports through the Amateur Athletic Foundation of Los Angeles. Due to this economic windfall, a direct result of the LAOOC's successful and commercial approach to sponsorship and marketing of the Los Angeles Games, they are considered to be a watershed for the corporatization of the Olympics. (Reich, 1986; Andranovich et al 2001).

Conclusion

People have used sport as a political tool in many ways and at many times. It would be naïve to expect that the Olympic Games be immune to this intrusion. How effective this interference is has been varied and often criticized. In judging whether or not the Olympic boycotts of 1984 and 1988 should have been instigated, what needs to be questioned is their total effect, not just on governments, but also to athletes, NOCs and the Olympic movement. Implicit in such calculations is the fact that, at some point in their sporting life, most athletes and sporting organizations have benefited from government funding, either directly or indirectly through the use of facilities, subsidies and sport science expertise. The Moscow and Los Angeles boycotts were obviously part of the whole Cold War diplomatic arsenal. Since that time there have been many changes to the main protagonists. The USSR has been dismantled and is now no longer communist and the US has itself fought in Afghanistan, as part of what President Bush terms 'the war against terrorism'.

The IOC has been placed under many different political pressures since this time, however Olympic boycotts have not been used as a weapon to the same extent since. Whether they are again implemented in the Olympic arena to such an extent remains to be seen. While Hill (1996.p. 36) notes that 'the IOC has not sought political involvement, but has it thrust upon it... It believes that political questions must be set by politicians, so its leaders frequently protest against the use made by politicians of sport, while themselves being obliged to act politically', others, such as Toohey and Veal (2000) argue that the IOC is overtly political. For example its campaign to promote the Olympic Truce seems to be a move into the area of international diplomacy. As such it can expect ongoing attention from political leaders.

References

Andranovich, G., Burbank, M. & Heying, C. (2001). Olympic Cities: lessons learned from mega-event politics, *Journal of Urban Affairs, 23(2),* 113-132.

Australia Olympic Federation (1979). *Annual Report.*

Australia, Parliament, 1978-1980, Debates (Representatives), Vol. H. of R. 111,

Australia, Department of Home Affairs (1980). *1979-80 Annual Report.*

Australia, Report to the House of Representatives Standing Committee on Expenditure, (1984). Payment to Athletes and Teams Who Did Not Participate at the 1980 Moscow Olympics.

Cohen, B. (1980). *Olympic Gold*, unpublished document.

Fraser, M. (1980). *The Moscow Olympics: The Case for a Boycott*, unpublished document.

Gordon, H. (1994). *Australia and the Olympic Games*, St Lucia, Queensland: University of Queensland Press.

Hill, C. (1996). *Olympic Politics* 2nd ed., Manchester: Manchester University Press.

Hill, C. (1999). The Cold War and the Olympic Movement. *History Today, 49(1),* 19-26.

International Olympic Committee (2001). Olympic Charter, http://multimedia.olympic.org/pdf/en_report_122.pdf

Lester, G. (1984). *Australians at the Olympics*, Sydney: Lester-Townsend Publishing.

Reich, P. (1986). *Making it happen. Peter Ueberroth and the 1984 Olympics*, Santa Barbara, CA: Capra Press.

Senn, A. (1999). *Power, politics and the Olympic Games*, Champaign, IL: Human Kinetics.

Toohey, K. & Veal, A. (2000). *The Olympic Games: a social science perspective*, Oxon, CABI.

Walton, A. *Olympic boycotts. In propaganda war, refusing to play is a risky move.* CNN Interactive, http://www.cnn.com/SPECIALS/cold.war/episodes/20/spotlight/

Vinokur, M. *More Than a Game: Sports and Politics.* http://www.mtholyoke.edu/~skcurtis/alaone.html.

AN INTERNATIONAL SPORT FEDERATION CASE STUDY: SOFTBALL

Peggy Kellers

Introduction

Sport governance is a multifaceted area that has an impact on sports at many different levels. For the sport of women's softball, its main focus during the past 40 years has been at the international level, specifically the Olympics. The main sport governing body that softball had to pursue in its quest to become an Olympic sport was the International Olympic Committee (IOC). Working through the International Softball Federation (ISF) and mostly by the effort of the Amateur Softball Association's Executive Director, Don Porter, softball had to take significant steps to secure advocates and allies as it rose to international prominence among a number of different countries.

Prior to 1962, the handful of countries that sponsored softball was essentially separate entities with no real international focus or stage. In August 1962, for the first time at a "world" softball tournament, there were two international entries, Japan and Canada that joined the 17 teams from across the United States to compete for the crown. Held in Stratford, Connecticut (USA), sponsored by the Amateur Softball Association (ASA), and hosted by the Raybestos Brakettes, the enthusiasm for softball had an added dimension that year. People's appetites were whetted as to the possibilities for softball at an international level. Looking on was the Australian Council, in addition to officials from Canada, Japan, and the United States. These representatives met during the tournament to discuss the feasibility of expanding softball's horizons and the possibility of sponsoring an international event. The rest is history.

Correspondence to: Peggy Kellers, Ed. D.,Associate Professor, James Madison University
MSC 2302, Harrisonburg, VA 22807, USA, Tel: +1 540 568 6514 Fax: +1 540 568 3338
Email: kellerpx@jmu.edu

Once a concerted effort was made to provide international softball competition and to help countries sponsor and develop softball, everyone's sights were set on the steps necessary to gain access into the Olympics.

If a specific sport wants to pursue competition at the Olympic level, the sport governance picture is neither a clear-cut process nor a matter-of-fact procedure. On paper, it may appear to be understandable and logical but, in reality, a variety of factors impact the decision by the IOC to add a sport to the Olympic Program. For the sport of softball, it took almost 31 years from the first sanctioned international championship (Australia, 1995) until the first game played in the Olympics (Atlanta, 1996).

Historical Perspective
In February 1965, at a time when the Olympic movement was once again going through significant turmoil and facing potential changes, the sport of fast pitch softball made a significant move on the international scene. Melbourne, Australia was the site of the first Women's World Fast pitch Softball Tournament. Five countries competed for the coveted prize of being named "World Champions". In addition to promoting one of the most popular women's team sports, the ultimate goal was to position softball in such a way that it would soon become an Olympic sport.

"Soon" on the international scene, and specifically in the Olympic movement, carried a much different time frame than most people, particularly Americans, understood it to mean. In June, 1991, when the official notification came that softball would be on the Olympic Program in the 1996 Olympic games in Atlanta, the dream became a reality. Along the way, many significant events and competitions took place. Thanks to the consistent effort of the ISF and ASA, fast pitch softball made its mark.

What were the steps that were taken to get to Atlanta, and what was the bigger picture as the softball world waited and watched for signs of hope and an official word of acceptance? The first question can be answered in more factual, quantifiable terms and from a fairly objective perspective. Answering the latter question presents a much more subtle, subjective, and often misunderstood frame of reference.

Frequently, on the international scene, overcoming the biggest challenges and obstacles requires quiet, unseen maneuvers strategically made in a climate of politics and gamesmanship among international powers. The politically savvy gain and understand that perspective, but to the passionate athletes, coaches, and fans, the wait seems unfair and, at times, it seems as though nothing is being done. "The ox is slow but the ground is patient" is a saying that is appropriate for this scenario. In retrospect, it may have been much easier if that saying had been etched in the minds and hearts of softball enthusiasts rather than the term "soon" during the 25-year wait for softball to be voted in as an Olympic sport.

Development of Softball as an International Sport—Steps to a Dream
Although softball began in 1887 in the United States and held its first international type competition in 1962, the impetus for the first World Championship came from the Australian Women's Softball Council, in conjunction with Canada, Japan and the United States. The well-established ISF (1952) became much more active as a result of this push from the Australian's (Littlewood, 1998). Along with the ASA, the ISF supported the Australian effort and officially sanctioned the ISF Women's World Championship. These championships have continued every 4 years at different sites throughout the world. In the first two championships, the host country won (Australia, 1965; Japan, 1970) with the United States being runners-up in both events. In 1974, the United States hosted (Stratford, Connecticut) and won the third championship and went on to dominate the international scene, a trend that has continued to the present time, with the exception of 1982 when the USA finished fourth. Several countries have emerged and challenged the United States dominance and the competitive gap is quickly closing with each international event (see Table 1). For the 1990 ISF World Championship, the United States changed the way their representatives were chosen and began having national team selections under the auspices of USA Softball, a newly established unit in the ASA.

Table 1. Results and participants of the ISF World Championships. Adapted from Babb (1997) and www.internationalsoftball.com.

Year and Venue	Results and Participants
1965 Australia	5 teams Australia (Gold), United States (Silver), Japan (Bronze) New Guinea, New Zealand
1970 Japan	9 teams Japan (Gold), United States (Silver), Philippines (Bronze) Australia, Canada, China, Mexico, New Zealand, Zambia
1974 United States	15 teams United States (Gold), Japan (Silver), Australia (Bronze) Bermuda, Canada, Republic of China, Italy, Mexico, Netherlands, New Zealand, Philippines, Puerto Rico, South Africa, Venezuela, Virgin Islands
1978 San Salvador	15 teams United States (Gold), Canada (Silver), New Zealand (Bronze) Australia, Bahamas, Belize, Chinese Taipei, El Salvador, Guatemala, Italy, Netherlands, Nicaragua, Panama, Puerto Rico, Virgin Islands
1982 Chinese Taipei	23 teams New Zealand (Gold), Chinese Taipei (Silver), United States (Bronze) Australia, Bahamas, Belgium, Bermuda, Canada, Columbia, Dominican Republic, El Salvador, Guam, Guatemala, Indonesia, Malaysia, Nauru, Netherlands, Nicaragua, Panama, Philippines, Singapore, Sweden, Venezuela
1986 New Zealand	12 teams United States (Gold), China (Silver), New Zealand (Bronze) Australia, Canada, Chinese Taipei, Indonesia, Italy, Japan, Netherlands, Puerto Rico, Zimbabwe
1990 United States	20 teams United States (Gold), New Zealand (Silver), China (Bronze) Argentina, Aruba, Australia, Bahamas, Bermuda, Canada, Chinese Taipei, Cuba, Indonesia, Italy, Japan, Netherlands, Netherlands Antilles, Mexico, Philippines, Puerto Rico, Zimbabwe
1994 Canada	28 teams United States (Gold), China (Silver), Chinese Taipei (Bronze) Australia, Canada, Cuba, Czech Republic, Italy, Japan, Netherlands, Netherlands Antilles, New Zealand, Puerto Rico, South Korea, Argentina, Bahamas, Belgium, Bermuda, Botswana, Columbia, Croatia, France, Great Britain, Moldova, Spain, Sweden, Ukraine, Austria
1998 Japan	17 teams United States (Gold), Australia (Silver), Japan (Bronze) Canada, China, Chinese Taipei, Columbia, Czech Republic, Italy, Netherlands, Netherlands Antilles, New Zealand, Philippines, Korea, South Africa, Venezuela, Denmark
2002 Canada	16 teams United States (Gold), Japan (Silver), Chinese Taipei (Bronze) Australia, Canada, China, Cuba, Czech Republic, Dominican Republic, Italy, Netherlands, Netherlands Antilles, Puerto Rico, Russia, South Africa, Venezuela

In the early stages at the international level, each country had autonomy as to how it would select players and coaches for the ISF Women's World Championship. The United States, for example, conducted a well-established, highly competitive national tournament each August to determine a National Champion. In 1963, the Raybestos Brakettes won and represented the United States at the first tournament. In 1966, the Brakettes were successful and represented at the Pan American Games. In 1969, the Orange Lionettes won and represented at the second tournament in Japan and in 1973, the Brakettes again won the National Championship and represented the United States at the third tournament, on their home field. If they had lost, it would have meant they watched another United States team host the World Tournament and compete as the United States representative. Being National Champions in the United States was a significant achievement but winning the year before the next world tournament had a special meaning and reward.

With each country's ability to develop its own unique selection process, some chose to select the best players to form their national team. For example, when Japan entered the softball scene, it chose an approach that required financial support from their government as well as a significant commitment in time and personal sacrifice for its athletes, coaches and softball personnel. Tryouts were held approximately one year prior to the championship. Those young women, including alternates (substitutes), went to a live-in camp for six months prior to the championship. Their training regime and sacrifices were extensive. At least eight hours or more a day was devoted to physical training, practice and competition. The discipline was rigorous, including limits on how much time players could spend with their family.

The age level of the athletes also varied. Within the Japanese culture during that time, it was rare for a woman to continue in athletics past the age of 20 or 22, which was when she typically settled down to raise a family. The Japanese, Philippines, and Chinese were typically much younger in comparison to the United States, Australia, and Canada. With few exceptions, those teams had members in their 20s, 30s and 40s.

In the United States, for example, at least five members of the ASA Hall of Fame (Rosie Adams, Joan Joyce, Peggy Kellers, Donna Lopiano, and Willie Roze) began their softball careers on nationally competitive teams prior to 16 years of age and continued into their late 20's or longer. Once again, athletes tended to hold on to the dream of being an Olympian by postponing their retirement. Even the athletes who began in the 1970s were unable to hold out, with the exception of three (Sheila Cornell, Dot Richardson, and Lisa Fernandez). In addition, as softball was an amateur sport, the older women had fulltime jobs and frequently had to take time off without pay and/or use vacation time in their devotion to playing softball. For many women who chose to be teachers, they had summers off and more freedom to spend their time playing softball.

One man, Don Porter, ASA Executive Director, became the consistent, stable force behind the scenes, and his tireless and unselfish contributions were significant in achieving this end. In a golden moment when the IOC President met with Don Porter in 1968 at the Olympic games in Mexico City, he got a glimpse of the road ahead. He heard President Brundage say, "Young man, softball is a great American pastime. I played it myself in Chicago, but it has a long way to go to make the program of the Olympics. You must develop it as more than an American sport and you must have patience" (Babb, 1997, p. 19). This IOC President, who was coming to the end of his difficult 20year tenure, was known for a bias against team sports and an opponent of women's participation in the Olympics (Senn, 1999). [If he had still been alive in the 1990s, what would he have said when his great granddaughter was named as an alternate to the United States' first softball team in the Olympics?] Although Don Porter did not necessarily want to hear what President Brundage said, it gave him an important component and a key link as to what to do next with softball (Babb, 1997).

During the same decades (1960s, 1970s and 1980s) the ISF was successful at getting softball recognized on the Pan American Games Program. In 1967, as an exhibition sport, the Raybestos Brakettes from Stratford, Connecticut represented the United States in the Pan American Games held in Winnipeg, Canada. This was to be a major step for softball in becoming part of the next Olympics. Although the United States dominated the other teams in this exhibition sport and easily won the Gold Medal, the Olympic dream was put on hold.

As a member of that team, this author was thinking that inclusion for softball into the 1972 Olympics was imminent and had planned the dates on a 1972 calendar. When one is focused on a dream, it is difficult to comprehend the difference between a realistic perspective and wasted energy. It was not until 1978 that softball became an official sport at the Pan American Games and "patience" continued to be the mode for softball at the Olympic level.

Thanks to the tremendous sponsorship by William S. Simpson, President and CEO of the Raybestos Manufacturing Company, more doors opened. The Raybestos Brakettes served as goodwill ambassadors on a number of occasions, doing clinics and exhibitions in many countries in the 1960s and 1970s including Holland, Italy, Zambia and Canada. It was also at this point that Ralph Raymond, Manager of the Raybestos Brakettes, emerged on the international scene. He became the most successful, most winning, long-term coach for the United States on the international level. For his success, being named the Head Coach of the United States team for the 1996 and 2000 Olympics rewarded him.

Softball players and coaches were committed to giving back to the sport they loved and seeing softball grow throughout the world, both numerically and qualitatively. In 1974, Donna Lopiano, a recently retired All-American with the Raybestos Brakettes and future ASA Hall of Famer, coached the team from Italy that came to the world championship for the first time. The other countries were open, hungry, and receptive to the knowledge and expertise Americans were willing to share so that they could become competitive.

Although it may seem strange, a key component for the delay in softball's entry into the Olympics may have had to do with the countries that sponsored softball and initiated programs during this period or the visible absence of softball in some of the more powerful countries in the world. The growth internationally certainly added to the strength and popularity of a women's team sport but there was still a significant set of countries that did not sponsor softball, specifically in the Eastern Bloc. European countries as a whole were not quick to pick up the sport, with the Netherlands first, followed by Italy.

The behind the scenes strategies were being covered solely by Don Porter. According to Babb (1997), Porter attended every international meeting there was. Remembering the words, *you must be patient*, he read the situation as best he could, watched as others made good and bad moves on behalf of their sports, and learned valuable lessons in the process.

One of the key strategies to know at this level is balance. Balancing being seen and heard with being seen and silent is a skill that has to be developed. Balancing the sixth sense (hunches, feelings, perceptions) with what is being seen and heard is also a keen sense to develop. Balancing a position of pushing and making a move with the right timing and the right approach is a strategy that pays off in time. Balancing activity among allies and advocates while maintaining respect for adversaries and people in power is wisdom. Balancing the watching and waiting with the asking and being proactive is a posture that must be maintained. To be effective, one must be balanced in each of these areas. How is it learned? Time, maturity, patience, making quality philosophical decisions, approaching people with respect, watching others' failures and successes, and careful choice of strategies.

Visibility is a strange commodity. At times it is helpful while at other times it is harmful. Don Porter was visible in his concern for the bigger picture, yet invisible with his picture and passion for softball. He was visible in his caring for other people's interests and, when asked, was able to share his interests, needs and passion. He was mindful of a closed door, a door that was ajar that could be nudged open, and a door that was wide open. He was visible with his support for sports in similar situations but careful as to whether or not he chose their same strategy and path.

When you are visible, you can also become the target of criticism, of attack, of misunderstanding, or perceived as doing nothing or playing games. Porter had a resiliency that gave him the ability to withstand the visibility. For example, his life was threatened over a situation that arose between China and Chinese Taipei when the latter hosted the ISF World Championship in 1982 (Babb, 1997).

He also learned when the timing was right and the climate was ripe for nudges and outright requests. In conversations with Porter, especially when this author served as the Executive Director of the National Association for Girls and Women in Sport (NAGWS), whose parent group (American Alliance for Health, Physical Education, Recreation and Dance) was a community-based member of the USOC, he had a good sense of the timing of the moves that had to be made. During this author's tenure at NAGWS (1989 – 1993), he knew that it was time to expand the letters of support on behalf of softball. This author wrote to several key IOC members, including the two US members and an IOC member from Finland and Canada. It was a personal thrill to have been not only an advocate as a player but also at the opposite end of the spectrum as an advocate from the ISF perspective. Once the official word came in 1991, the United States and seven other countries began to prepare the patient, well-oiled machine of softball for the 1996 Olympics. In the end, patience does bear fruit.

The Bigger International Picture: Challenges, Delays and Obstacles in Softball's Journey to the Olympics

History provides a great perspective and somewhat clear picture. What happens amongst leaders at the top is very often reflective of what goes on at the grassroots levels. In other words, attitudes and beliefs usually turn into actions and behaviors, whether they are politically, socially, athletically, culturally, or nationally motivated.

The question, "Could it be...?" is frequently asked within a system based upon power and influence when someone is trying to figure out and piece together information, especially in times of delays when there are no clear answers. It may be similar to what a physician goes through when s/he is trying to diagnose a patient's condition. There are facts, procedures, experiences, risks, hunches, questions, the known and unknown, decisions, and finally, there is reality and the sense that this is "the way it is". In looking at the bigger picture, one can ask "Could it be...?", but because of the complex nature of the Olympics and the many factors that impact it, the answer usually is speculative at best. What was going on not only in the overall Olympic movement but also in the world during the 1960's, 1970's, and 1980's may have had a major impact on the delay softball experienced in becoming an Olympic sport.

Amidst the Cold War, racial discrimination (e.g. apartheid), the demise of Communism, terrorist attacks, wars, and as a result, several boycotts of certain Olympic Games, the IOC faced major decisions and controversies beyond selecting new sports for the Olympic Games. During the three decades from the 1960's to the 1990's, the possible "Could it be...?" scenarios will be highlighted to catch a glimpse of the bigger picture that was staring the sport of softball in the face.

"Could it be...
- Philosophy, position and posture of the IOC leadership?"

Avery Brundage (USA) served as IOC President from 1952 – 1972. He assumed the position immediately following a brief four-year stint of Mr. Edstrom (Sweden) who tried to re-ignite the Olympic movement after a 12-year break surrounding WWII. As a pacifist, Edstrom believed strongly that sport could offer the world a new and better moral code. Although his efforts were short-lived, he stepped into a situation that had developed in the Olympic movement during the 1930s, at a time when the Germans had significant power in the IOC and professionalism and commercialism had already taken root. Brundage wanted to restructure the Olympics to reflect Coubertin's foundational beliefs. Team sports and women were not part of the first Olympics in Athens, Greece. In fact, it was not until the 1900 Paris Olympics that men's soccer made the program. Therefore, team sports should be dropped and women's events should be dropped or at least reduced (Senn, 1999). Although his ideas were not supported, it could be a big reason for the delay.

- The issues surrounding the participants within the sport?"

Increasing female representation at the Olympics has been a slow, uphill battle. Table 2 gives a clear picture of the low percentage of females and female sports during the time that softball was requesting its entry. In addition, the newest glitch faced by the IOC was the emergence of performance-enhancing drugs and "men" competing as women. Was there a subtle fear that this problem could escalate by adding softball?

Table 2. Male and Female participation at Olympic Summer Games.
Adapted from Senn (1999) and Blue (1988) and www.olympic.org.

Year	Male Athletes	Female Athletes	Total Athletes	% of Female Participation	Female Sports	IOC President
1896	311	0	311	0	0	Coubertin
1900	1319	11	1330	0.83	5	Coubertin
1904	681	6	687	0.87	1	Coubertin
1908	1999	36	2035	1.77	2	Coubertin
1912	2490	57	2547	2.24	2	Coubertin
1920	2543	64	2607	2.45	2	Coubertin
1924	2956	136	3092	4.40	3	Coubertin
1928	2724	290	3014	9.62	4	Baillet-Latour
1932	1281	127	1408	9.02	3	Baillet-Latour
1936	3738	328	4066	8.07	4	Baillet-Latour
1948	3714	385	4099	9.39	5	Edstrom
1952	4407	518	4925	10.52	6	Brundage
1956	2958	384	3342	11.49	6	Brundage
1960	4738	610	5348	11.41	6	Brundage
1964	4457	683	5140	13.29	7	Brundage
1968	4750	781	5531	14.12	7	Brundage
1972	5848	1299	7147	18.18	8	Brundage
1976	4838	1247	6085	20.49	11	Killanin
1980	4201	1125	5326	21.12	12	Samaranch
1984	5511	1567	7078	22.14	14	Samaranch
1988	6279	2186	8465	25.82	17	Samaranch
1992	7855	2708	10563	25.64	19	Samaranch
1996	7118	3626	10744	33.75	21	Samaranch
2000	6582	4069	10651	38.20	25	Rogge
2004	6452	4412	10864	40.61	27	Rogge

- The male counterpart sport is yet part of the Olympic Games?"

Another factor may be that it took baseball 25 years to become an Olympic sport. As the so-called male counterpart to women's softball, and in a male-dominated leadership and participation, maybe baseball had to be ushered in first (Los Angeles, 1982) before softball could gain access.

- Key countries in the voting have yet to sponsor the sport?"

The mix of countries that played and did well at softball may have been a deterrent for the IOC members during those three decades. It seems that a voting member would not fully understand the value and excitement of a sport if s/he had not been associated with it. As the Olympic movement became more politically motivated, the common question in the political arena is "what's in it for me?" or in this case, "my country?"

- Lack of women and minority men in voting positions at the IOC?"

The IOC Executive Board manages its affairs and has responsibility for the Olympic Charter. They have been slow to model the importance of having women and minority men involved in the power positions. "The *(Olympic)* Congress also recommended that more women participate in Olympic institutions and in the IOC, but the IOC was slow to follow the *(Olympic)* Congress' recommendation" (Senn, 1999, p. 162). Killanin, although aware of the sentiment, ended his term as IOC President by not naming any woman to the IOC (1972 – 1980). It was not until Samaranch became IOC President that two women were named to the IOC (Senn, 1999).

Controversy Surrounds the Chosen Governing Body

The IOC has the sole authority to recognize international sport organizations as the governing body within the Olympic movement. The ISF is the official governing body for softball at the international level. The United States Olympic Committee (USOC), as an IOC member, has the authority to name the governing body within the United States for each Olympic sport. For softball, USA Softball, under the ASA umbrella, is the National Governing Body (NGB). Prior to the Olympic games of 1996 and 2000, serious controversies erupted about softball's NGB. Although the ASA has been the main organization to carry the torch for softball, questions continue to loom as to their commitment to truly follow the Olympic Charter. Specifically, the question of why women and minority men are not represented at all levels of the organization is the dark cloud that hangs over the ISF and the USA's NGB. The most recent challenge has come from a newly formed organization, Softball America (National Fast pitch Coaches Association website). They want to have a strong voice and a vote in the affairs that impact their sport at the national and international level.

Although similar questions were asked at the IOC level in the 1970's and 1980's, some positive changes have been made. The NGB has not, however, followed the same pattern. This issue is the newest focus for softball.

It was a special thrill for the Hall of Famers and many long-time softball enthusiasts to be at the Softball Venue of the Olympic games in 1996. This author and the others watched with great anticipation and quiet reflection as the sounds of "Let the Games begin" echoed throughout the stands. The reunion of what was once again the pioneers and the opportunity to meet with those athletes who would reap what was sown was exceptional. It was history in the making and everyone had a deep sense that this one did not come easily or quickly. What does the future hold for the Olympic sport of Softball? Only time can tell the story. For this generation of women softball players, perhaps their experience and lesson in patience will be worth it to see women and minority men step into positions of power and influence in the decision making structure of the ISF, USA Softball, head coaching positions, and the director of national programs position.
"The ox is slow but the ground is patient."

References

Babb, R. (1997). *Etched in gold*. Indianapolis, IN: Masters Press.

Blue, A. (1988). *Faster, higher, further*. London, England: Virago Press.

International Olympic Committee (2000). *Olympic Charter*.

Littlewood, M.L. (1998). *The path to the gold*. Columbia, MO: National Fast pitch Coaches Association.

Plummer III, B. (2000). *Amateur Softball Association Softball's Hall of Famers*. Norman, OK: Transcript Press.

Senn, A.E. (1999). *Power, politics, and the Olympic games*. Champaign, IL: Human Kinetics.

www.internationalsoftball.com - Events section of the International Softball Federation website.

www.olympic.org - Homepage of the International Olympic Committee website.

www.nfca.org – Home Plate on the World Wide Web.

ELITE SPORT DEVELOPMENT AND NATIONAL TEAM SELECTION: A HONG KONG PERSPECTIVE

Pak-kwong Chung

Introduction

Hong Kong is a cosmopolitan city, known as one of the leading financial and trading centers of the world. As the gateway to Mainland China and with China's accession to the World Trade organization, Hong Kong's efficient port, quality management and market knowledge has made the city even more important to global investments.

Although Hong Kong is one of the most densely populated cities, accommodating 6.8 million people within a total land area of 1098 square km, its government funded recreation and sporting facilities have never been stifled as result of land restriction. According to Government figures (see http://www.info.gov.hk), the total number of recreation and sports facilities in 2001 was 1715. Details of Hong Kong's Recreation and Sports activities and facilities are presented in Table 1.

Compared with recreation and Sport for All, elite sport in Hong Kong receives less support from the Government. This support includes financial resources and policies conducive to the development of elite athletes, such as the provision of an educational system and career opportunities. The huge disproportion between the Government's funding allocating to recreation and Sport for All and elite sport is reflected in the 2002/03 budget allocation, where, which are 2260.5million HKD (about US$290.5million) and 189.7million HKD (about US$24.3million) were allotted respectively. Thus, elite sport represents only 7.7% of total funding.

Correspondence to: Pak-kwong Chung, D.P.E., Director of Elite Training and Sports Development, Hong Kong Sports Development Board, Email: pkchung@hksdb.org.hk

The Government has traditionally paid less attention to elite sport because of the historically international status of Hong Kong, which went from a colonial city to a Special Administrative Region (SAR). It is a city where emphasis lay on financial and commercial achievements and where patriotism and national pride brought from sport excellence seemed less valued by society. This situation remained the same until 1996 when Hong Kong achieved a gold medal at the Atlanta Olympic Games. Elite sport suddenly became the focal point. Government and the public began to realize that international sporting achievement could not only raise the international profile of Hong Kong, but also strengthen the public's loyalty and sense of belonging. As a result, elite sport immediately received additional financial support. This incident also exposed the reality of elite sport, whereby– results are not everything, but the *only* thing, as they are the yardstick for success or failure.

Sport Delivery System in Hong Kong
In the sport delivery system of Hong Kong, the SAR Government plays a key role in the structure of activities, ranging from mass participation to training at elite levels. The Government's policies on sport and recreation are coordinated by the Home Affairs Bureau, with a number of expert bodies contributing to the development of these policies, including the Hong Kong Sports Development Board, the Leisure and Cultural Services Department, the Sports Federation and Olympic Committee of Hong Kong, China, and the National Sports Associations. Figure 1 represents the system graphically.

Figure 1. *New Sports Structure in Hong Kong.*

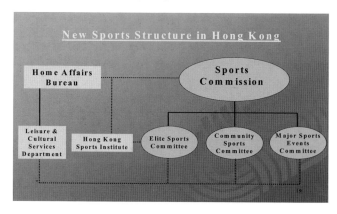

Sports Federation and Olympic Committee of Hong Kong, China

The Amateur Sports Federation and Olympic Committee of Hong Kong was founded in 1949-1950 and recognized as a National Olympic Committee in 1951. It changed to the present name of the Sports Federation and Olympic Committee of Hong Kong, China (SF&OC) in 1999. The SF&OC is responsible for organizing Hong Kong's participation in major games such as the Olympics, Asian Games, and East Asian Games. With the support from its 72 National Sports Associations members, the Federation also organizes many sports activities which promote the Olympic movement in the community.

National Sports Associations

The National Sports Associations (NSAs) are affiliated with their respective International Federation (IF) and are managed by elected officers under either limited company or registered society ordinances. They are responsible for promoting and organizing a wide range of activities specific to their sports, including coaching programs for participants from beginner to elite level, local and overseas competitions, and training courses for coaches and referees. Although each organization has its identity and scope of responsibility in the delivery system, each NSA makes their best efforts to accommodate differences amongst one another for the sake of providing a conducive environment for Hong Kong sports to grow, develop and pursue excellence.

Leisure and Cultural Services Department

The Leisure and Cultural Services Department (LCSD) is a Government agency created in January 2000 to replace two provisional municipal councils (urban & regional councils). The LCSD aims to develop and manage recreation and sports facilities and to organize a wide range of leisure activities in the community. The total budget from the Government in 2002-2003 was 2,260.5million HKD. The facilities and activities managed by the LCSD are presented in Table 1.

Table 1. Recreation, Sports Activities and Sports Facilities in 2001.

Recreation and Sports activities	
No. of recreation and sports activities organized	24,170
No. of participants in recreation and sports activities	1,361,712
No. of physical fitness activities organized	8,615
Type of Recreation and Sport facilities	
swimming beaches	36
children's playgrounds	610
natural and artificial turf pitches	71
hockey pitches	2
rugby pitches	2
hard surfaced pitches	217
holiday camps	4
major parks	22
indoor games halls/leisure centers/indoor recreation centers	82
sports grounds	24
squash courts	324
stadia	2
swimming pool complexes	36
tennis courts	265
water sports centers	4
bowling greens	9
golf driving ranges	5

Hong Kong Sports Development Board

The Hong Kong Sports Development Board (SDB), established in 1990, was the statutory body responsible for the development of sport and physical recreation in Hong Kong. In 2002-2003, the Board received a government subvention of $189.7 million HKD (US$24.38 million), which included a contribution to the Elite Training Program for Hong Kong's top athletes at the Hong Kong Sports Institute (about $13.88 m USD in 2001/2002).   The Board was also responsible for allocation of governmental funding to 55 National Sports Associations (about $16.07 m USD in 2001/2002).

In May 2002, the Home Affairs Bureau (HAB) of the Hong Kong Government released the report of the Sports Policy Review Team, entitled "Towards a More Sporting Future", for public consultation. The Report identified the key issues that need to be addressed in drawing up a strategic policy for Hong Kong's future sporting development. It also helped generate discussion among the stakeholder groups on the desired way forward.

At the conclusion of the 2-year consultation exercise, HAB proposed to create a new administrative structure for sports, recommending that SDB be replaced with a Sports Commission to act as a high level advisory body for sports development, and to follow up on the recommendation and feedback received in relation to the Report.

The Sports Commission (SC)

The SC consists of three Committees to help develop and promote community sports, elite sports and major sports events in Hong Kong with a view to realizing the new vision for sports development, so:

(a) A sustainable and community-wide sporting culture whereby people of all age groups participate actively in sports in quest of sound physical and psychological health, as well as positive community spirit.

(b) A cadre of high performance athletes who can compete in major international and overseas sports events competitively, and become role models for our youth.

(c) Hong Kong becomes an attractive venue for hosting international sports events of different nature and size, thereby brining in more tourists and other economic benefits.

The three Committees, comprising representatives from different sectors with the relevant expertise and experience, will recommend policy initiatives and priorities in annual resource allocation in their respective area for consideration and endorsement by the SC.

The three Committees are:

(a) Community Sports Committee – to advise the Administration through the SC on wider participation in sports through closer partnership with different sectors of the community, and on funding priorities for supporting community sports programs and initiatives;

(b) Major Sports Events Committee – to advise the Administration through the SC on strategies and initiatives to facilitate the hosting of major sports events in Hong Kong through close collaboration with sports associations, tourism industry, and the private sector, and on funding priorities; and

(c) Elite Sports Committee – to advise the Administration through the SC on matters pertaining to high performance sports, provide policy direction to the future HKSI, and on funding priorities for supporting high performance sports and athletes.

Table 2. *Terms of Reference for the Sports Commission Committees.*

	Terms of reference – To advise the Administration on:
Sports Commission	• the formulation of a sports policy for sports development in Hong Kong; • the building of partnership relationships among major stakeholders in sports in Hong Kong, in order to facilitate the effective implementation of the sports policies; and • the broad principles and guidelines in the provision of funding support to sports and related organizations for promoting and developing sports in Hong Kong.
Community Sports Committee	• the strategies and initiatives to promote community participation in sports, other than elite sports, having due regard to the needs of people of different age, gender, ability and other background and those with a disability; • the strategies to foster partnership with different sectors of the community for the promotion of community sports; • the interface with relevant authorities on the integrated framework for development of student sports, including curriculum-based and co-curricular activities; • the development of community sports clubs and their interface with District Sports Associations and NSAs; • the promotion of major community sports programs; • the principles, procedures and the control mechanism for subventing and sponsoring community sports; and • the funding priorities for community sports programs.
Elite Sports Committee	• the strategies for providing elite training programs for HKSAR athletes with a view to achieving international sporting success; • the development of partnership relationship with different sectors of the community and sports training institutions, both local and in other places, to enhance the delivery of elite sports training programs; • the coordination and mobilization of stakeholders in the sports sector and in the community at large to provide support to elite athletes including their personal, educational and vocational development; • the strategies to promote sponsorship and participation of the private sector in elite sports development; • the policy direction of the Hong Kong Sports Institute including coach education and accreditation; • the principles, procedures and the control mechanism for allocation of funds of elite sports; and • the funding priorities for elite sports development.

Table 2 cont...

Major Sports Events Committee	• the strategies and initiatives for the promotion and hosting of major sports events in Hong Kong; • the strategies to foster partnership with the sports, tourism and private sectors for major sports events; • the principles, procedures and the control mechanism for allocation of funds for major sporting events; and • the funding priorities for major sports events.

Elite Sport Development

The Jubilee Sports Centre

The transition from the amateur to professional management of elite sports began in 1982 when the Jubilee Sports Centre (JSC) was opened to implement the raising of sports performance standards in Hong Kong and to increase participation in sports and recreation.   The Center, located in Shatin, New Territories, with 41 acres of reclaimed land, was a jointed development project by the Government and the former Royal Hong Kong Jockey Club (now named The Hong Kong Jockey Club).   In order to achieve higher standards of performance, the Center provided top-class training facilities to 10 selected sports: Athletics, Badminton, Basketball, Fencing, Gymnastics, Squash, Soccer, Swimming, Table-tennis and Tennis.   The sports were selected based on considerations of physique, the climate of Hong Kong, inherent attitudes and cultural doctrines, as well as characteristics that keep Hong Kong athletes pursuing sporting excellence. In the initial set up, the Center provided indoor facilities, including 3 sports halls, 11 squash courts, a 25m swimming pool, residential accommodation for athletes and visitors, weight training room, restaurants, coaching and administration offices.   The outdoor facilities consisted of a cycling velodrome, an athletics track, 9 tennis courts, 3 soccer pitches, 6 basketball courts, 4 volleyball courts, a covered sport training track, and jogging trail.   (Current facilities are essentially the same.   See http://www.hksdb.org.hk).

Before the JSC was established, elite training and development were the responsibility of the individual NSAs. After the JSC took responsibility for elite training of selected sports, conflicts resulted between the Centre and some of the selected sports NSAs. This was a controversial aspect of the Center's work and was interpreted in some quarters as trespassing on the autonomy and independence of the voluntary sports movement. The policy at that time was unique and had no precedent in Britain (until 1997, Hong Kong was a British colony). However, through regular dialogues and communication, practice in the development of elite athletes and services provided by the Center was accepted by most NSAs. As suggested by Jones (1988), having the Centre as the employer for coaches indeed had advantages, with uniform conditions of service, specific job descriptions and monitoring of performance established.

The Hong Kong Sports Institute
In 1988, the Government made a commitment to endorse the proposals in the *The Way Ahead,* a consultancy undertaken by E.B. Jones on the status of sport in Hong Kong. In the report, the consultant suggested the JSC, which took the Crystal Palace National Sports Centre in London as a model in the initial building, should be made comparable to the Australian Institute of Sport for future expansion and development. It was also suggested that the sport science and the Hong Kong Institute of Sports Medicine be developed and housed at the Centre. At an extraordinary meeting on 2 September, 1988, the Board of the Centre agreed to expand its influence to become an institute of sport and the conceptual and financial effects of this were addressed.

After fulfilling the required legislative procedures, the Center's name was formally changed to the Hong Kong Sports Institute (HKSI), effective 1 April 1991. The mission of the HKSI is to provide an environment in which athletic talent can be identified, nurtured and developed. The objectives of the HKSI are: Athlete development and management, Coach education and development, Sport science, Sports medicine and research, resources information, international exchange and cooperation with other bodies. Building upon the solid foundation laid down by the JSC, the HKSI expanded its scope of work in an effort to provide comprehensive and integrated support services to the elite athletes supported at the Institute.

Through unfailing support produced by the JSC and then the HKSI in working with the respective NSAs, and the full commitment of athletes and coaches, Hong Kong Sports finally received a payback and earned the respect, not only from the local people, but also the world after Ms Lee Lai San, a windsurfer, won the first Gold medal for Hong Kong in the Olympic Games held in Atlanta, USA in 1996.

When considering the limitations faced by Hong Kong in developing elite sports, the Gold medal achieved in the Olympic Games was a remarkable accomplishment.   The success also served as a milestone for the development of Hong Kong elite sports. Another breakthrough came at the 1998 Bangkok Asian Games, in which Hong Kong athletes captured 5 Gold, 6 Silver and 6 Bronze medals. The historical result ranked Hong Kong 13th among 41 countries in the medal standing. Previously, the last and only Gold was won in 1986. Other sporting achievements in major games in the past ten years are presented in Table 3.

Table 3. *Medal Achieved in Asian Major Games by Hong Kong Athletes 1992 – 2001.*

	Asian Games			Commonwealth Games (before 1997) All China Games (after 1997)			East Asian Games		
Year	G	S	B	G	S	B	G	S	B
1992									
1993							1	2	7
1994		6	7			3			
1995									
1996									
1997						1		1	5ª	4ᵇ
1998	5	6	6						
1999									
2000									
2001				2	2	1	3	4ᶜ	8ᵈ

a : including 3 from demonstration events
b : including 2 demonstration events
c : including 3 from demonstration events
d : including 5 from demonstration events
Remarks : Hong Kong Disable Sports have also achieved distinguished results at Paralympics, Far East and South Pacific Games for the Disabled and World Championships in past years.

In 1991, based upon a report commissioned by the Government, efforts began to integrate the SDB with the HKSI. The integration was designed to provide a more efficient and effective service to sport, yet allow the identity of the HKSI to be preserved and its vital role in producing top athletes. The integration was completed on 1 April 1994. The administration of the elite training, originally supported by the HKSI, comes under the responsibility of the Elite Training Group in the new SDB structure.

Another recommendation of the "Towards a More Sporting Future" report was that HKSI be re-constituted to concentrate on the development of high performance sports, provision of coaching and coach education upon its eventual detachment from the SDB. The recommendation was approved in the Legislative Council on 9 June 2004. Under HABs arrangement, SDB was dissolved on 30 September 2004 and the new sports structure was fully implemented on 1 October 2004.

The newly re-constituted HKSI has become an incorporated body to allow greater flexibility in its management and operation. Working under the endorsed policy direction of the Sports Commission, the future HKSI will be a delivery agent for high performance sports services currently under the auspices of the SDB; i.e., management of high-performance athlete training programs, coach training and education, training of junior and pre-elite squads, and provision of performance – related information and research projects. In addition, the future HKSI will maintain liaison with its counterparts outside Hong Kong, especially those in the Mainland, with a view to exploring scope for closer collaboration and exchange. It will continue to be financially supported by the Government through annual subvention allocation.

Selection of Elite Sports

The Concept of Elite Sports
It is impossible for a country to excel in every sport at the elite level. The concept of "medal sports", "Elite sports", or "Focus Sports" is a worldwide practice in the competitive sports field. Hong Kong has focused its resources on selected sports since the JSC opened in 1982, when10 sports were selected and supported at the Centre. As selected sports receive more resources and benefits, many NSAs aim to be selected as "Elite Sports". It now seems, however, that no single yardstick can be used to perfectly measure all sports, as each sport has its uniqueness to be promoted and developed. As a result, debates and disputes occur each time a selection process takes place. In order to find a better solution to the selection criteria for elite sports as well as a more reasonable funding mechanism to support all NSAs, the SDB Board established a "Special Review Sub-committee for Sports Support" to conduct a review in 1999. The review was completed in 2000 and after full consultation with all stakeholders, a new set of selection criteria was implemented.

The Selection Criteria for Elite Sports
In the new criteria, sport achievement is the only yardstick used for the assessment. Original factors such as the NSAs performance on administration and organization of training programs for athletes and officials, access to training facilities, community appeal of the sport, and NSAs partnership with SDB, were removed. On the professional sport circuit, results are the only thing that justifies whether the sport deserves more funding or investment regardless of the support from Government or commercial sectors. Compared with other factors, competition results are more objective in the assessment. In the present selection criteria, a general scoring table is established (Table 4). Scoring ranges from 1 – 5 points, with achievement at the Olympic Games, Asian Games, or World Championships carrying the highest points. Considering that the competitive level of Olympic Games is still beyond what some Hong Kong athletes may actually achieve, the Asian Games and World Championship achievement is given the same ranking as the Olympics.

The achievement of senior athletes carries more weight than that of juniors, considering that the competitive level is higher in senior events. Similar to practice in most Asian countries, only those Olympic Games or Asian Games recognized sports are considered as Elite or Focus Sports in a governmentally funded support system. The selected sport is supported as an Elite Sport for a 4-year cycle. Evaluation is conducted every two years to provide opportunity for other sports to be elevated as well as assess performance of the existing Elite Sports.

Currently there are 13 Sports supported in the Elite Training Program of SDB: Athletics, Badminton, Cycling, Fencing, Rowing, Squash, Swimming, Table-tennis, Tennis, Tenpin Bowling, Triathlon, Windsurfing and Wushu. Each elite sport is in residence at the HKSI and receives support in the areas of coaching, travel expenses for training and competitions, sport facilities and equipment, sport science and sports medicine services, athlete stipends as well as education and career development. There were approximately 300 athletes, including senior and junior, in the program in the 2002-03 financial year.

Table 4. Selection Criteria for Elite Sports

Item / Weight	Criteria	Rating				
1 / 1.5	International level performance record in previous 2 years – Senior athletes	4-8 (>24 entries) or Top 1/3 (≤24 entries) International Invitation Tournament Regional Champs (e.g. Pacific Games) International Open	4-8 (>24 entries) or Top 1/3 (≤24 entries) East Asian Games Asian Cup World Cup	4-8 (>24 entries) or Top 1/3 (≤24 entries) Asian Champs All China Games World University Games/ Champs	4-8 (>24 entries) or Top 1/3 (≤24 entries) Olympic Games Asian Games World Champs	Medal Olympic Games Asian Games
		Medal (>9 entries) or Top 1/3 (≤9 entries) Interport / Inter-City Competition **[1 point]**	Medal (>9 entries) or Top 1/3 (≤9 entries) International Invitation Tournament Regional Champs (e.g. Pacific Games) International Open **[2 points]**	Medal (>9 entries) or Top 1/3 (≤9 entries) East Asian Games Asian Cup World Cup **[3 points]**	Medal (>9 entries) or Top 1/3 (≤9 entries) Asian Champions All China Games World University Games/ Champs **[4 points]**	Medal (>9 entries) or Top 1/3 (≤9 entries) World Champs **[5 points]**
2 / 1	International level performance record in previous 2 years – Junior athletes	4-8 (>24 entries) or Top 1/3 (≤24 entries) International Youth Invitation Tournament Regional Youth Champs International Youth Open	4-8 (>24 entries) or Top 1/3 (≤24 entries) World Youth Cup	4-8 (>24 entries) or Top 1/3 (≤24 entries) Asian Youth Champs All City Games	4-8 (>24 entries) or Top 1/3 (≤24 entries) World Youth Champs World Youth Games	Medal (>9 entries) or Top 1/3 (≤9 entries) World Youth Champs World Youth Games
		Medal (>9 entries) or Top 1/3 (≤9 entries) Interport / Inter-City Youth Competition **[1 point]**	Medal (>9 entries) or Top 1/3 (≤9 entries) International Youth Invitation Tournament Regional Youth Champs International Youth Open **[2 points]**	Medal (>9 entries) or Top 1/3 (≤9 entries) World Youth Cup **[3 points]**	Medal (>9 entries) or Top 1/3 (≤9 entries) Asian Youth Champs All City Games **[4 points]**	

Requirements for Results to be Considered

1. Due to lack of uniformity in various sports disciplines, international ranking will not be used as an assessment parameter.
2. Only performance results of competitions which are sanctioned by the relevant IF/AF will be recognized.
3. For Olympic Games and Asian Games medal achievements, the "minus-one rule" will be applied. Please explain the minus one rule
4. Only achievements for events with 4 countries/regions taking part will be counted.
5. Achievements of demonstration events of competitions will not be counted.
6. Results of individual events achieved by the same athlete in both senior and junior events will only be counted in either category.
7. For team sports, inter-clubs competitions, whether local or international, will not be used as an assessment parameter.
8. Only achievements of athletes fulfilling the 3 year residency criteria will be counted.

National Team Selection

It is standard practice that the determination of selection criteria for a national team or delegation to participate in Olympic Games (as well as Asian Games and East Asian Games in Asian countries) shall be the responsibility of the National Olympic Committee (NOC), in collaboration with their National Sports Associations or Federations. As suggested by the International Olympic Committee (IOC), the application of the selection process should be the responsibility of a NOC selection committee which applies the criteria with fairness, impartiality, and adherence to the rules.

According to the IOC policy and guidelines for NOC Team selection, stated in the Sport Administration Manual (IOC, 1999), the NOC undertakes the selection of an Olympic team openly, with as clean and objective criteria as possible. The process will be closely monitored by all, including the media. It must be fair from the perspective of the athletes, their coaches, and their sport federations. The following are guidelines suggested by the IOC (1999):

1. The selection process should be as objective as possible, utilizing international results to help determine the ranking of the athlete in the world. Athletes can qualify as eligible for the Olympic Games in the 12 month period proceeding the games, thus giving the athlete and coach

assurance well before the games, and allowing training to be focused on the games rather on selection trials just proceeding the games.

2. Criteria for selection for a sport should be negotiated between the NOC and the national sport federation two to three years before the Games.

3. The NOC must consider the athletes nominated by the national federation. There may be circumstances where an athlete is eligible, but not selected. For example, if a rowing crew qualifies before the games, then a substitution is made and that substitution is nominated by the national federation, then the original rower in the crew would not go to the Games.

4. If selection has been made on a discretionary basis, the selectors should keep a brief written record of the grounds for the decision.

5. After the selection has been announced, a representative of the selection committee should be available for a 48-hours period to explain the basis of decision according to the written record.

6. If within 48 hours of the decision, and after speaking with the committee representative, the athlete believes that grounds for appeal exist, the athlete should submit a formal appeal, clearly stating the reasons why he or she should have been selected.

7. A selection appeals board, composed of two national board members who did not sit on the selection committees, plus an elected athletes' representative who did not sit on the original committee, should consider the athlete's statement, plus a statement from the selection committee representatives and make a decision within 24 hours of receipt of the appeal, and notify all parties concerned.

In Hong Kong, National team selections for participation in Olympic Games, Asian Games, and East Asian Games are conducted by the Sports Federation and Olympic Committee of Hong Kong, China (SF&OC). The selection criteria used to select the national teams to take part in the 14th Busan Asian Games held in Korea in 2002 included athlete's achievements in the preceding Asian and World Championships, the East Asian Games, and the 9th All China Games, and those who have qualified for the 2000 Sydney Olympics or demonstrated outstanding performance in 2001. Athletes were also required to pass a medical check to demonstrate fitness for competition. The preparation plan of their respective members of the NSAs were also taken into consideration in the selection process.

According to the Olympic Charter (1997), the selection of athletes and teams must (a) respect the spirit of fair play and non violence, and behave accordingly on the sports field; (b) refrain from using substances and procedures prohibited by the rules of the IOC, the IFs or the NOCs; and (c) respect and comply in all aspects with the IOC Medical Code.

Conclusion

Although Hong Kong is an international financial center, recreation and sport play an important role in improving the quality of life for the people of Hong Kong. The success of Hong Kong athletes in the 1996 Atlantic Olympic Games has proven that a small and densely populated city like Hong Kong has the ability to compete with other countries in prestigious multi-sport games. The success has also raised the public's awareness and expectation for elite sports. However, the weak sports culture, strong academic-oriented school curriculum and, uncertain career prospects after sport are still the major barriers for elite sport to move forward. Another challenge is how concerned parties can work together in harmony towards a common goal, which is to provide the best environment and support system to help talented athletes pursue sporting excellence. The economic downturn is also an important factor that may reduce the funding from both the Government and commercial interests. Interestingly, Beijing has won the bid to host the 2008 Olympic Games. Hong Kong, as part of China, will do its best to nurture elite athletes so that the SAR flag can be raised at many medal presentation ceremonies during the 2008 Beijing Olympics.

References

Hong Kong Sports Development Board. (2000). 10th Anniversary Commemorative Brochure.

Hong Kong Sports Development Board. (1995). Annual Report 94/95.

Hong Kong Sports Institute. (1991). Souvenir Book: JSC to HKSI – The evolution of the Jubilee Sports Centre to Hong Kong Sports Institute.

International Olympic Committee. (1999). *Sport Administration Manual.* Olympic Solidarity, International Olympic Committee.

Jones, E.B. (1988). *The Way Ahead – A Consultancy Report on Sport in Hong Kong.*

COMPLIANCE WITH BEST PRACTICE GOVERNANCE SYSTEMS BY NATIONAL SPORTING FEDERATIONS IN SOUTH AFRICA

Salmar Burger, Anneliese Goslin & Mollie Painter-Morland

Introduction

In earlier times, governing sport seemed to be less troublesome and complex than it is today. Originally, both national and international sports governing bodies were established to codify rules and organize events and tournaments. Their role later expanded; they encouraged, promoted and subsequently facilitated international exchange between other sports governing bodies. However, this rapid globalization and commercialization of sport has created a host of new competing interests (Katwala, 2000; Australian Sports Commission, 1999), resulting in various stakeholders within the sphere of sport who now challenge the ability of sport to govern itself (Governance in Sport Working Group, 2001). This increased attention from politicians, legislators and governments reflects a growing recognition of the importance of sport, the impact of sport and the role it plays in modern society, culture, the economy and politics. The heightened interest, however, carries the risk of legislative over-regulation of sport. Even though legal intervention is not a risk *per se*, intervention leading to regulatory and statutory compliance requirements as a result of under-performance may potentially undermine the principles of flexibility and self-regulation that has been central in the development of sport thus far (Governance in Sport Working Group, 2001). The changed status of sport (economic role-player and increased professionalization and globalization) increasingly forces it into the business sector. As such, sport will have to comply with best practice corporate governance systems applicable to the business sector to avoid regulation.

Correspondence to: Sálmar Burger; Department of Biokinetics Sport and Leisure Sciences, Centre for Leisure Studies, LC de Villiers Sport Centre, University of Pretoria, 0002, South Africa E-mail: salmar.burger@up.ac.za

This chapter aims to present an overview of best practices governance systems and justifies the need for such practices in modern day sport. Compliance to the principles of good governance of South African national sports federations will be presented and discussed.

Sport as a Player in the Economic Sector

Viewed from a business perspective, sport is currently highly global and successful. The Olympic Games held in 2000 in Sydney, hosted 10,300 athletes from 200 countries competing in the various events. Sponsorship expenditure exceeded US$600 million and spectatorship amounted to US$3.7 billion globally (Katwala, 2000). In South Africa, sport also plays an undeniable role in the economy. The most recent economic indicators show that the total contribution of sport to the South African GDP (including capital expenditure on sport) is placed at 2.1% or ZAR16,765 million. Additionally, the South African sports industry provided an estimated 34,325 full-time positions in the labor market, 6140 part-time positions and an estimated 8000 volunteer workers. An overall sport industry growth of 32.35% occurred over the period 1997-1999 (South African Sports Commission, 2000). Although two major capital expenditure sport projects, namely the 7th All Africa Games and the Pakisa Motor Raceway in Welkom, contributed to this figure, it remains a considerable growth.

It is clear that sport makes a significant contribution both monetarily and in terms of job creation to the South African economy. In doing so, sport is responsible for managing quite substantial amounts of funds either through government grants or sponsorships. The average annual total contribution from the commercial sector to South African sport amounts to ZAR2,291 million (South African Sports Commission, 2000). The inability of sport to ensure at least an acceptable return for the investor often leads to withdrawal and loss of substantial and much relied on private sector funding for sport.

This was clearly demonstrated in the case of Athletics South Africa (ASA) who had within a period of five months, lost its two main sponsors, namely ABSA Bank (The Editor, 2003a) and Engen, a South African petroleum company, who ended the sponsorship "due to a need for the company to focus more on Corporate Social Investment initiatives and pressure on existing sponsorship to demonstrate return on investment, presumably the ASA sponsorship was not delivering on Engen's objectives" Rakhale, (2003b: online).

A major advantage of a well-governed sport body lies in its ability to attract and retain sponsorship in a sustainable way. Adherence to sound business principles aids in attracting additional funding, ensuring longer-term sustainability and identifying and managing inherent risks (Van Heerden, 2001). Sports federations are increasingly obliged to increase their levels of professionalism and governance principles necessitated by the higher economic demands from the sponsorship and advertising sector. Good governance contributes to limiting potential future liability and exposure to future risk alike (Naidoo, 2002; PricewaterhouseCoopers, 2003). Lost sponsorship might also result from of a lack of sufficient high-level management attention being given to non-financial matters. The recent media response to alleged racism within South African rugby just prior to the 2003 Rugby World Cup, illustrates this issue. The article, headlined "Boks: Sponsor concerned" reports that the main sponsor of the Springbok rugby team expressed concern about the developments around the racism allegations (News24, 2003). It is specifically stated that the sponsor has "requested the South African Rugby Football Union to handle matters in a proper and professional manner" (News24, 2003: Online). Financial loss and even total financial collapse pose major risks for any organization and sport body alike. Bush Bucks, a South African soccer club has been relegated from the Castle Premiership and placed under provisional liquidation due to liabilities amounting to ZAR14 million and financial ruin is immanent without financial rescue in the form of newfound sponsorship (Rakhale, 2003a). Unless South African sport federations do not succeed in demonstrating competence in self-regulation, legislative intervention might be imposed, as was the case of Boxing.

Legislation was imposed on Boxing as a result of financial mismanagement. The Internet site, Business Through Sport, reported in this regard as follows: "Two years ago [2000] the activities of Boxing South Africa were suspended following financial mismanagement, which rendered the organization dysfunctional. The new legislation, signed into law by President Thabo Mbeki, has paved the way for the establishment of a body that is expected to administer boxing with a greater degree of professionalism" (The Editor, 2002).

The Need for Best Practice Governance Systems in South Africa
Sport and the governing structures of sport are not above the law. Yet in South Africa, fewer legal rules and requirements are applicable to sports bodies than those applicable to corporate bodies and other legal and regulatory entities. Legislation regulates almost every aspect of corporate business, but from a legal point of view sport *per se* remains largely unregulated at this time.

The issue of governance in South African sport has already received some attention at the government level. In a parliamentary media briefing on 12 September 2001 the incumbent Minister of Sport and Recreation, M.N. Balfour stated: "The current state of affairs in a number of national federations is characterized by in-fighting [and] a perceived lack of unity. In taking these factors into consideration, it has become crucial for Government to ensure that these situations are reversed. The amendment to the [Sports Commission] Act is a transparent process whereby Government wants to ensure good governance in South African sport" (Balfour, 2001).

Given the increasing number of scandals and crises being reported in the media today, good governance in sport is becoming increasingly important. The common thread linking these kinds of controversies seems to be a questionable application of best practice governance principles, rather than commercialism (Katwala, 2000).

The Salt Lake City Olympic Games controversy, the Tour de France scandal of 1998, the Hansie Cronje Cricket investigation, the fraud charges and subsequent convictions of officials within South African Boxing circles during the 1980s as well as the alleged South African Rugby racism debacle prior to the 2003 Rugby World Cup, resulted from dubious application of governance principles (Pretorius, 2003; Van der Berg, Munasamy & Schoonmaker, 2003; Van der Berg & Padayachee, 2003).

The Australian Sports Commission (2002b) contends that the decline in performance experienced by Athletics Australia during the second half of the 20th century, the inability of the athletics federation of Australia (Athletics Australia) to adapt to increasingly demanding business environments. After major changes to its governance systems was introduced, dramatic improvements were recorded in financial performance and business success over a period of five years (1997 - 2002) with a five-fold increase of value-in-kind income over a three year period (1999 - 2002).

Sport has an undeniable role in society, with discernable effects on the political, social and economic fronts. "Sport can be a tool of dictatorship or a symbol of democratic change - it can help to start wars or promote international reconciliation. Sport can't bring about social change by itself - but it can be a powerful symbol and catalyst for changes in national identity, gender roles and race relations." (Katwala, 2000). It might be for this reason why a wide spectrum of stakeholders commits private and public funds to sport. Governments and the private sector across the globe fund the development of sporting infrastructures, due to the perceived potential benefits sport may bring about. Enhanced stakeholder activism puts pressure on sport federations to implement the principle of self-regulation. Unless sports bodies can demonstrate an ability to competently and responsibly govern themselves, they run the risk of the national legislature issuing legislation that may contain a number of new, expensive and even highly cumbersome requirements to be adhered to. Sports bodies should voluntarily comply with best practice standards in terms of governance if they wish to avoid becoming highly legalized and formally regulated. To prevent the necessity of legislation to enforce good governance, sport and its sports bodies must develop their own rules and guidelines for proper governance, based largely on principles already proven in the business sector.

Good governance in sport makes good business sense (Naidoo, 2002). Long-term sustainability depends on this and further aids the generation of additional funds, implementation of sustainable growth strategies and management of sport within agreed business parameters so as to limit potential liability (PricewaterhouseCoopers, 2003; Naidoo, 2002).

Development of Corporate Governance
Globally, corporate governance has received growing interest over the past decade and several authoritative publications on governance principles have appeared (Foreman, 2001). Even within the international sports industry, governance issues surfaced when the first international conference in sport governance took place in Brussels in February 2001 (Governance in Sport Working Group, 2001).

The starting point of corporate governance came in the early 1990's with the formation of the Cadbury committee in the United Kingdom (Gaved, 2001). The subsequent publication, 'Report of the Committee on the Financial Aspects of Corporate Governance' in December 1992, provided a governance model and framework for many other countries on which to build and formalized the field of corporate governance (Wilkinson, 2003; Gaved, 2001; Reed, 2000; Steele, 1999; Stapledon, 1998). The institutionalization of corporate governance in South Africa came with the publication of the first King Report on Corporate Governance (King I) in November 1994 (Institute of Directors, 1994; Wilkinson, 2003).

Global and local interest in corporate governance has lead to efforts to codify various principles and policies. The overarching themes of the majority of these are to ensure responsible and accountable long-term and short-term operations by organizations. These codes have evolved to describe the governance of organizations by broadly advocating the pursuit of the following actions:

- The creation of best practices to ensure accountability of actions, responsibility by the organization, and transparency towards its broader societal stakeholders;
- This will lead to the greater propensity for assuring that organizations comply with legal and regulatory obligations;

- The creation and monitoring of checks and balances to ensure that the exercise of power within an organization is balanced;
- The effectuations of a process whereby risks are identified that threaten the sustained existence of an organization within the accepted parameters.

2002 King Report on Corporate Governance for South Africa

The 2002 King Report on Corporate Governance for South Africa (King II) was published in March 2002 (Institute of Directors, 2002). According to Naidoo (2002) the report is founded on the notion that any contextual manifestation of governance should reflect the societal value system within which it is based. The King II Report identified the need for an uniquely African, and even more importantly, South African business culture which stood to be created and incorporated African value systems that emphasizes: "...the collective over the individual good; the principles of mutual interdependence and co-existence; the spirit of humanity (*ubuntu*), which is based on the premise that the individual is entitled to respect only because of his cordial coexistence with others; a hierarchical political ideology, but one based on an inclusive system of consultation at various levels; a preference for consensus over dissension; and a mentality of inherent trust and belief in the fairness of human beings." (Naidoo, 2002,13)

Specific areas covered by the King II Report were expansions of the first King report in 1994. Apart from abovementioned incorporation of African values and ideals of *ubuntu* (humanity towards others), additional concepts such as integrated sustainability, organizational integrity, stakeholder engagement, and triple bottom line reporting have been included in the King II Report (Institute of Directors, 2002). In terms of its status, King II only serves as a guide to ideal states of good governance, especially for those organizations falling outside the report's jurisdiction. Also, it is not feasible to expect national sports federations, or any membership association for that matter, to adhere to all of the recommendations that The King II Report embodies in the archetypical corporate governance standard. However, because the principles do apply, the 'inspirational' effect is important. Applicability of this is not *bona fide* as the physical structuring of membership associations differ from that of corporate enterprises.

However, The King II Report is built on certain fundamental principles described as the 'Pillars' of good governance. These principles do find universal applicability (Naidoo, 2002) and in this sense hold the same inherent value for any corporate enterprise and sports federation alike.

Sport Governance Code – 2001

The majority of Best Practice Governance codes and guidelines are aimed at governance within the corporate or commercial sector with a number specializing within specific corporate sectors, such as investment, insurance or auditing.   Within sport, there has also been an attempt to codify principles of good governance. In February 2001, a conference aimed specifically at discussing the issues of governance in sport was held in Brussels.   A draft document titled "Statement of Good Governance Principles for Sports Governing Bodies" was issued (Governance in Sport Working Group, 2001).   The conference report states that sport is increasingly attracting attention from politicians, legislators and courts in Europe. Inherent risks in the form of legislative or judicial intervention that could potentially undermine the flexibility of self-regulation within sport in general are emphasized.   The report furthermore states that the European Council Declaration at Nice reaffirmed support towards the independence of sports controlling bodies and the right to self-regulation.   Such support however, was conditioned upon the premise that sports governing bodies observe principles of democracy, transparency, and solidarity across the industry and also adhere to a code of ethical conduct.   Sport should thus earn the benefit of having its "specificity recognized" (Governance in Sport Working Group, 2001: 3).   Failing to do so will pressure legislators, nationally and internationally, to intervene through the provision of statutory acts regulating sports bodies in a similar fashion to that of commercial enterprises.   The conference concluded that the substantial revenue generating ability of sport through broadcasting rights, sponsorship, and gate revenue should not detract sports governing bodies from the fact that the main objective of their existence is still founded in their primary obligation to promote their sport and increase participation at all levels. However, this implies the need for long-term sustainability as an inherent requirement for best practice governance. Through the gaining of insight into these simple principles and others identified in the conference, the fundamentals of best practices become evident.

Best Practice Governance Systems

The issue of governance and, more specifically, the term 'corporate governance' has succeeded in attracting widespread public interest in most developed economies over the past decade. This might be attributed to the apparent importance attached to the economic health of organizations and companies within society in general. Corporate governance has been broadly defined in various initiatives (Hampel Committee on Corporate Governance, 1998; Directorate for Financial, Fiscal and Enterprise Affairs, 1998) as being the relationship between management, the board of directors who have been appointed by owners to oversee the management of the company on their behalf and the shareholders themselves (Foreman, 2001; Commonwealth Association For Corporate Governance, 1999). The concept of 'corporate governance' might however be poorly defined because its scope is too broad in terms of the number of distinct economic phenomena it includes. The different application fields of management and business shade the interpretation given to the concept in those respective fields. This leads to yet more definitions being developed. Foreman (2001) proposes that contemporary use of the term "governance" relates to the role of the board in performing its oversight function of management. This is seen as a more proactive function to ensure sustainable performance for the legitimate owners.

In order to define exactly what constitutes best practice governance systems, various sources on this subject should be examined. An overview of the relevant literature reveals the following definitions of "corporate governance":

> "The simplest, most generally-accepted definition of governance is the responsibility and accountability for the overall operation of an organization" (DeGroote, 2000).

> "Corporate governance is the system by which companies are directed and controlled" (Cadbury Committee Report, 1992; <http://www.ose.no/cg/definisjoner_E.pdf>; <http://www.encycogov.com/WhatIsGorpGov.asp>).

"Corporate governance is concerned with holding the balance between economic and social goals and between individual and communal goals ... the aim is to align as nearly as possible the interests of individuals, corporations and society" (Cadbury, in Institute of Directors, 2002).

"The system by which companies are directed and controlled for the benefit of shareholders" (Steele, 1999).

"The responsibility and accountability for the overall operation of an organization" (Bohen, in Taylor, 2000).

OECD Principles of Corporate Governance (1999) - International organization "[C]orporate governance ... involves a set of relationships between a company's management, its board, its shareholders and other stakeholders. Corporate governance also provides the structure through which the objectives of the company are set, and the means of attaining those objectives and monitoring performance are determined.   Good corporate governance should provide proper incentives for the board and management to pursue objectives that are in the interests of the company and shareholders and [this] should facilitate effective monitoring, thereby encouraging firms to use resources more efficiently".   (Ad Hoc Task Force on Corporate Governance, 1999; <http://www.ose.no/cg/definisjoner_E.pdf>).

"Corporate governance encompasses the system of laws, codes and regulations that govern the way in which corporate organizations - including football clubs - behave and operate.   The system of corporate governance defines the rights and roles of different participants in an organization - the shareholders, the board of directors, employees and other stakeholders - and the relationships between them". (Hamil, Michie, Oughton & Shailer, 2002).

"Corporate governance is the system [by which] corporate entities (which include nearly all sporting bodies) are directed or managed and controlled" (Australian Sports Commission, 1999).

Even though most of these definitions are focused on corporations with a commercial interest, the principles of responsible, transparent, fair and accountable management toward all stakeholders central to this theme apply globally to all types of organizations, including sport organizations.

Pillars of Best Practice Governance

Gaved (2001) reports that improvements have been identified in the governance of organizations by boards and CEO's alike due to the new impetus in the requirement of boards to act in an accountable manner towards its stakeholders. These improvements are directly coupled to the introduction of higher and more uniform governance standards based on widely recognized and supported principles of ethical and fair behavior in the form of governance frameworks, "pillars of governance" or principles of good governance (Rossouw, de Koker, Marx & van der Watt, 2003; Wilkinson, 2003; Naidoo, 2002). These so-called pillars are based largely on expectations of increased accountability and transparency across every aspect of society. Furthermore, there is a growing intolerance of organizations and individuals who fail to demonstrate that they consistently follow the high standards that are expected of them (Gaved, 2001). The increased global and local focus on these most basic pillars has lead to efforts to codify various listed policies and codes. Through the identification of these codes, pillars have been expanded to include themes of responsibility, sustainability fairness and social responsibility (Foreman, 2001; Steele, 1999). In this regard Rossouw *et al.* (2003:3) concluded that currently "corporate governance hinges on four cardinal values: fairness, accountability, responsibility and transparency. Recommendations about board composition, directors' duties, risk management and internal audit are merely mechanisms for assuring that corporations adhere to these four cardinal values." The identified pillars of good governance will now be clarified.

ACCOUNTABILITY

The need for accountability receives extensive attention in corporate literature (Gerrard, 2003; Ozanian & Decarlo, 2003; Rossouw *et al.*, 2003; Wilkinson, 2003; DiPiazza, 2002; Football Governance Research Centre, 2001; Foreman, 2001; Gaved, 2001; Rauter, 2001; Taylor, 2000; Australian Sports Commission, 1999; Football Task Force, 1999; The

Institute of Chartered Accountants in England and Wales, 1999 and Hampel Committee on Corporate Governance, 1998). Attention is focused on accountability as an indispensable prerequisite for good governance by several codes and organizations (Institute of Directors, 2002; Governance in Sport Working Group, 2001; Australian Sports Commission, 1999; The Institute of Chartered Accountants in England and Wales, 1999; Directorate for Financial, Fiscal and Enterprise Affairs, 1999; Hampel Committee on Corporate Governance, 1998; Institute of Directors, 1994; Cadbury Committee Report, 1992; European Corporate Governance Institute: Online).   The need for accountability pertaining specifically to sport is identified and discussed by Ryan (2002), Gaved (2001), Foreman (2001), Rauter (2001) and Katwala (2000). Katwala (2000) unequivocally states that informal sports governing structures coupled with closed cultures have largely resisted the impetus to change and adapt to modernized views of the world and governance even though the sports industry is experiencing a decreased ability to cope with increasing corporatization and commercialization of globalized sport and also with the new found pressures of accountability and transparency. The creation of a culture of accountability flows from the need for accountability. Mere provision of information is not sufficient. An inherent commitment should accompany the act of accountability amongst the stakeholders and role players alike in the administration of sport and its governing bodies.   This, according to DiPiazza (2002) implies taking responsibility, which can only occur in the presence of an ethos that values, understands and supports accountability. Rauter (2001) adds that accountability and responsibility are linked as individuals responsible for actions or outcomes are held accountable for them.   However, accountability in this sense then also proposes that those individuals or role players delegating tasks or actions are also accountable for the actions and outcomes of the acting parties.   Only the responsibility to physically perform the actions can be delegated but not the accountability for these actions. This, if it were to happen, would constitute an abdication of accountability.

According to the Australian Sports Commission (1999), the board of a sports body is accountable to its legal and moral owners.   It has accountability to those with whom the organization has a business and a fiduciary relationship as well as a moral duty towards members and broad stakeholders (Foreman, 2001; International Governance in Sport Conference Report, 2001; Australian Sports Commission, 1999).

Accountability ultimately lies with those parties who make decisions, take actions and implement measures on specific issues thus providing means to query and assess the actions of the governing officers and committees (King, 2002; Naidoo, 2002; Commonwealth Association for Corporate Governance, 1999; Dine, 1995; Cadbury Committee Report, 1992).

RESPONSIBILITY

Responsibility as a pillar of good governance is clarified by Rossouw *et al.* (2003), Wilkinson (2003), DiPiazza (2002), Foreman (2001), Rauter (2001), Taylor (2000), Australian Sport Commission (1999), Football Task Force (1999), Directorate for Financial, Fiscal and Enterprise Affairs (1999) as well as the Hampel Committee on Corporate Governance (1998). The majority of governance codes do not distinguish between the concepts of accountability and responsibility, the assumption being that these are inextricably linked. Indeed, the term 'responsibility' is sometimes used interchangeably with 'accountability'. A description of the meaning of responsibility is offered by the Australian Sports Commission (1999) in proposing that each member of the governing board is responsible for all decisions taken by the board. This implies that board members share a common liability and they could be held legally liable both individually and collectively in the event of an alleged failure by the board to properly exercise its 'duty of care'. Ryan (2002) suggests that principles of effective governance should lead to a guarantee that the roles and responsibilities of role players and members of the sport body are clearly delineated so that individuals can work in closer harmony and achieve greater efficiency. This is necessary to ensure that available resources are put to the best use for the sport. Responsibility refers to "the obligation of the board to take good care of the assets" of the organization (Rossouw et al., 2003, 3). This involves both investments and stakeholder interests and implies that the responsible board will protect the organization's material assets and reputation from damage. Responsibility is regarded as behavior that allows for corrective action as well as penalization of mismanagement. Responsible management would, when necessary, introduce actions to direct the organization onto the correct path. Rossouw et al. (2003) describes this as providing stakeholders with recourse mechanisms in the event of sustaining harm due to the actions and behavior of the organization.

TRANSPARENCY

The need for transparency as a pillar for good governance is widely agreed on (PricewaterhouseCoopers, 2003; Rossouw *et al.*, 2003; Wilkinson, 2003; DiPiazza, 2002; Institute of Directors, 2002; Naidoo, 2002; Ryan, 2002; Foreman, 2001; Gaved, 2001; Governance in Sport Working Group, 2001; Rauter, 2001; Australian Sports Commission, 1999; Commonwealth Association for Corporate Governance, 1999; the Institute of Chartered Accountants in England and Wales, 1999; Directorate for Financial, Fiscal and Enterprise Affairs, 1999; Hampel Committee on Corporate Governance, 1998; Institute of Directors, 1994; Cadbury Committee Report, 1992). Some discussions of governance codes couple the principles of communication and disclosure either implicitly or explicitly with that of transparency. Essentially these terms are encompassed by the notion of transparency within the context of this discussion.

One particular view on transparency and disclosure of information and decision making is held by Rauter (2001), where the ideal governance system is described as unconcealed to the relevant stakeholders in terms of strategy, decision making and decision making principles and reporting on financial and operational performance.

Transparency and communication are key components in establishing legitimacy within an organization (Gaved, 2001). Effective communication requires great clarity in terms of the message being communicated, including provision of information in ways that are relevant and meaningful to the intended audience and includes the key values of openness and timelessness. Commitment to such communication in the organization should manifest itself in three visible ways that can be examined to gauge the extent of this commitment:

- The general communication framework and principles of the organization;
- The extent to which these have been developed and transformed to reflect the needs of the organization and its members;
- The tangible implementation of these principles within the organization.

In the absence of the latter way, issues of governance run the risk of being viewed as a paper exercise without any practical benefit or relevance (Gaved, 2001).

The way in which a sport governing body communicates with its members is a key indicator of the quality of its governance processes. Key aspects of communication, according to the guidelines established by the International Governance in Sport Conference Report (2001), include:

- A clear statement of the governing body's approach to governance and articulation of its responsibilities towards members;
- Regular communication with members on policy decisions, elections and other matters (executive, legislative, judicial, commercial); and
- Direct two-way communication providing channels for feedback from members.

Sport governing bodies are compelled according to these guidelines to regularly report formally to its membership-holding constituents on its activities, including a summary of the governing body's finances and financial activities. Frequent reports targeted at the needs of specific groups of members may be deemed appropriate in this regard. The Internet could be a most valuable instrument for this purpose to make information readily available to members, stakeholders and all interested parties.

The initial benefit of a transparent reporting system is to expose "political machinations, corruption and the bumbling amateurism of delegates" (Katwala, 2000), thereby opening all decisions of governing bodies to public scrutiny. This is important not only on a global scale, e.g. awarding the Olympic Games to a country, but also on a localized scale such as team selections and awarding of prizes by national and even provincial sport federations. Transparency is non negotiable.

Despite this principle of transparency, sports bodies sometimes tend to view these inquiries from stakeholders and in particular the media, as illegitimate, for example FIFA (International Football Federation) President Sepp Blatter's response to allegations of bribery: "The referee has blown his whistle. The players have left the field. The game is over" (Katwala, 2000).

In the final analysis, transparency (inclusive of the term disclosure) can be defined as the ease with which an outsider is able to make a meaningful analysis of the organization's actions, its economic management fundamentals, and the non-financial aspects pertinent to that organization. It is a measure of the success with which management makes the necessary information available in a candid, accurate and timely fashion - not only audit data but also general reports and press releases. It reflects ease in the ability to obtain a true picture of what is happening inside the sports organization.

SOCIAL RESPONSIBILITY
Social responsibility as a pillar of good governance refers to recognition of others' interest and realization of all stakeholders' needs. Sports federations are regarded as social entities and as such, actors within the broader society in which they operate. Their actions and decisions should therefore be beneficial to those individuals and groups directly involved in the federations as well as to the broader social environment. Social responsibility encompasses a social as well as an economic dimension.

In terms of the economic dimension of social responsibility, the South African National Sport and Recreation Act 110 of 1998 (South Africa, 1998b) states in Section 10 (1e) that the funding of sport and recreation, and in particular funding provided to national federations, is done under certain terms that "demand acceptable standards of administration from recipients of government funding".   Section 10(3) further states that granting of funding is dependent on the practice and exercise of a social responsibility in as far as exclusions occur based on discriminatory reasons. Exclusion of certain social groups as stakeholders in a broad social sense based on discriminatory reasons will disqualify sport federations from receiving government funding. Sports federations are further compelled to pro-actively participate in programs and institute actions to promote social and environmental needs and priorities. In addition, sports federation must recognize and pursue the aims of cultural and social cohesion through their sports, in particular, adherence to Section 9 of the South Africa Bill of Human Rights.

The social perspective of social responsibility brings the topical issue of HIV/AIDS in sport to the forefront. Sport federations are prohibited to discriminate against participants (stakeholders) with the disease and simultaneously address the issue of risk management to protect all involved stakeholders from possibly contracting the disease. According to Sankaran et al. (1999, 40) "with risk management being a hot topic in today's corporate and professional society, it is only a matter of time until those who organize and conduct recreational and competitive sports events feel the need to inform all persons involved with event management about universal precautions [against HIV/AIDS]."

At the International Governance in Sport Conference in 2001, proposals were tabled to increase sports federations' awareness toward interest groups outside the immediate ambit of the sport that are likely to be affected by its decisions and actions (Governance in Sport Working Group, 2001). Well-managed sport organizations are aware of and successfully respond to external and internal social issues and place a high priority on adherence to ethical standards. A good socially responsive and responsible entity is increasingly seen as one that is non-discriminatory, non-exploitative, and responsible with regard to both environmental and human rights issues.

INDEPENDENCE

Independence as a pillar of good governance refers to the extent in which measures and mechanisms have been introduced to minimize or avoid potential conflicts of interest that may arise within the sports federation (Rossouw et al., 2003; Strickwerda, 2003; White, 2003; Wilkinson, 2003; Institute of Directors, 2002; Naidoo, 2002; Rauter, 2001; Brown, 2000; Australian Sports Commission, 1999; Commonwealth Association for Corporate Governance, 1999. Gregory, online). These mechanisms may range from the composition of the Board to committee appointments by the Board and appointment of external parties, such as auditors. Any decision taken on the establishment of internal processes should be objective in nature and free from undue internal and external influences.

As governing bodies occasionally get involved in one or more of the commercial aspects of sport, conflict of interest may arise where the wider interests of the sport may not necessarily be reconcilable with the specific commercial objective. To prevent this, the Governance in Sport Working Group (2001) recommended that there should be a clear demarcation between the governing body's governance function and any commercial activities or involvement. This demarcation can be achieved by allocating differentiated roles to respective committees or bodies within the governing body. In such a case each committee or body must have clearly defined responsibilities and chains of reporting. The committee or body dealing with commercial responsibilities should, whenever appropriate, consider an open tender system for awarding any contracts. Rauter (2001, 1) holds the view that independence implies "independent views and opinions, objective assessment and freedom from constraints of internal and external influence".

Governing bodies must be able to justify all actions and decisions through a process of rational reasoning. In addition, procedures must exist for resolving differences. Such procedures might include access to internal or external appeals, access to arbitration (whether ad hoc or through a recognized body such as the South African Sports Commission) or a combination of such procedures. In all cases, procedural fairness, transparency, accessibility and efficiency should be central to the process. No individual in a decision-making capacity on an arbitration or appeal board or panel should have any interest or stake in the outcome of the dispute. To ensure fair access to such procedures, a governing body should do nothing to hinder a party from seeking remedy under the present judiciary system of the country.

FAIRNESS

Fairness is inherent to the ethos of sport participation. Fairness as a pillar of good governance dictates that internally created management systems within organizations should take equitable account of all those stakeholders with a legitimate claim in the interests and future of such an organization (Rossouw *et al.*, 2003; Wilkinson, 2003; Institute of Directors, 2002; Naidoo, 2002; Football Governance Research Centre, 2001; Brown, 2000; Australian Sports Commission, 1999; Commonwealth Association for Corporate Governance, 1999 and Directorate for Financial, Fiscal and Enterprise Affairs, 1999). The importance of fairness in the governance of South African sport is emphasized by Section 13 of the National Sport and Recreation Act No 110 of 1998 (South Africa 1998b). The section states that the South African Sports Commission is entitled to take action should uncertainty exist about the standards of management. In particular, the Commission may implement actions or take steps to ensure adherence to the principles of discipline and fairness (South Africa 1998). The board of a sports governing body has a moral obligation to consider all matters on the basis of equity and transparency and in the interests of the sport as a whole, and not in preference to any one or more classes of stakeholder (Australian Sports Commission, 1999).

Internationally, sports governing bodies recognize that fair and effective distribution of financial revenues from the sale of commercially valuable rights related to sports events encourage the development of talent and contributes to balanced and attractive competitions. This should also be the case in national and regional sports bodies. In the light of increasing commercialization and the resulting regulatory and political review of the structures and organization of sport, a clear policy for the redistribution of income is essential. Sports governing bodies should therefore adhere to the following general principles as guidelines for fair redistribution of revenue (Governance in Sport Working Group, 2001; Brown, 2000):

- Redistribution must be based on principles of solidarity (between all levels of the sport), while adhering to governmental and other regulatory guidelines;
- Redistribution policies must pursue aims that are objective and justifiable;
- Effective communication through all levels of a sport is essential;

- Administration of redistribution mechanisms must be transparent, accountable and objective.

Fairness at the level of a national sport federation thus implies giving due consideration to the interests (including issues of race and gender) of all relevant stakeholders - not only those who stand to gain from involvement, but also those who are in danger of being disenfranchised due to a lack of direct contact and relations with the governing sports body. Rossouw *et al.* (2003) state that an unbalanced make-up of board executives may lead to decisions favoring the inherent biases of the majority of representatives. If the governing board of a sports federation is composed mainly of technical training personnel such as coaches, decisions relating to long-term sustainability might, for example, be renounced in favor of short-term goals of on-field performance.

DISCIPLINE

Discipline as a pillar of good governance represents a commitment by the senior management of the organization on behalf of its members to adhere to behavior that is universally deemed correct, acceptable and proper (Rossouw *et al.*, 2003; Wilkinson, 2003; DiPiazza, 2002; Institute of Directors, 2002; Naidoo, 2002; Commonwealth Association for Corporate Governance, 1999). Disciplined behavior and commitment are reflected by:

- Demarcation and separation of responsibilities between the governing body, its board and other parts of the organization;
- The holistic structure and organization of the governing body and the sport;
- Selection and appointment of members to the governing body;
- Limitation of terms for elected representatives;
- Adherence to an ethical policy.

Current Compliance to the Principles of Good Governance in South Africa

The management paradigm of the majority of South African sports federations has shifted from amateur sport to professional sport. This shift placed sport federations in the business sector and performance is now benchmarked against good governance principles. A number of recent management controversies in sport, as well as demands from private and public sector funders, initiated a study to measure compliance with good governance principles, as discussed above. From an extensive literature study on corporate governance, the following main pillars/dimensions, as well as sub-elements of each pillar emerged. These are outlined in Table 1.

Table 1. *Summary of identified good governance principles.*

Pillar/Dimension	Sub-elements
Accountability	Accountability Structure, responsibility and accountability
Responsibility	Structure, responsibility and accountability Responsibility
Transparency	Transparency Transparency and communication Website efficacy
Social responsibility	Social responsibility Recognition of other interest
Independence	Free from outside influence Objectivity Decisions and appeals Conflicting interests
Fairness	Democracy, elections and voting Nominations Fairness Solidarity
Discipline	Discipline Role of the governing body Ethical policy

A first attempt was made to determine the level of compliance to the identified principles and sub-elements of best practice governance of 36 South African sports federations from a total of 90 federations. Provisional findings of this study are shown in Table 2 and a copy of the instrument used can be found in the Appendices.

Table 2. *Compliance to best practice governance elements by 36 South African Sports Federations (provisional).*

Pillar of best practice governance	Average compliance (%)
Accountability	73.92
Responsibility	65.96
Transparency	66.38
Social Responsibility	72.13
Independence	64.70
Fairness	72.27
Discipline	59.89
Collective compliance	67.89

From this study, it has become evident that national sports federations in South Africa need to give particular attention to the dimensions of responsibility, transparency, independence and discipline. In the case of transparency, it holds great importance for sports federations' future ability to attract and retain sponsorship. Sponsors, as well as government, increasingly require greater transparency and openness regarding the application of their funding. If sports bodies cannot competently prove responsible and transparent behavior they stand the chance of losing additional income streams. The relative low compliance with independence as a pillar of good governance manifests in the inability to take autonomous and fair actions. It seems as if federations and governing bodies in South African sport are not as objective as they should be nor are they free from conflicting interests. This implies that decisions and actions might not always reflect the best interest of the federation or not adequately consider long-term implications of short-term actions.

The low level of compliance with best practice standards around discipline indicates that sport federations need to improve the implementation of ethical policies and review the functioning of governing bodies. Sports federations that are regarded as undisciplined run the risk of a damaged reputation, which may result in a loss of sponsorship.

Formalized guidelines as suggested by the King II Report may be required to assist South African sport federations in the transition from amateur sport to professional sport governance. If sport is to avoid future regulation, then attention must be given to the implementation of systems to ensure that principles of good governance are more prevalent with federations.

Conclusion

Pressure on National Federations is mounting to ensure that there is a system of strong governance principles in place not only to protect the long-term stability and survival of the organization (Rauter, 2001; Australian Sports Commission, 2000b; Australian Sports Commission, 1999), but also to maintain an equitable balance between international development and adherence to the way in which local participation is managed. Adhering to a clearly defined set of governance principles, specifically in sport, carries the following benefits (Governance in Sport Working Group, 2001):

- It is useful in determining responsible behavior towards members and other legitimate stakeholders;
- Demonstrates that all actions and decisions are properly motivated and subjected to appropriate checks and balances;
- By exhibiting self-regulation virtues, inhibiting legislative interference into the matters of sport can be minimized.

A well-managed sport organization must be aware of, and respond to, social issues, and place a high priority on ethical standards. It requires recognition of all relevant stakeholders associated with the national sports federation that are likely to be affected by decisions and actions. This embodies the recognition and pursuit of cultural aims and social cohesion through sport, also through the adherence to the Humans Rights Bill in terms of equality. South African sports federations should be increasingly seen as non-discriminatory, non-exploitative, and responsible with regard to environmental and human rights issues. The ethical imperatives yield significant benefits in terms of improved productivity and corporate reputation, which in turn result in increased investor confidence and sponsorships. Good governance should therefore be a firm priority of all South African sports federations.

References

Ad Hoc Task Force on Corporate Governance. (1999). Internet: <http://www.ose.no/cg/definisjoner_E.pdf> 15 March 2003.

Australian Sports Commission. (1999). *Governing sport: the role of the board and CEO.* ASC Publications: Sydney.

Australian Sports Commission. (2002a). *Governance in surf life saving Australia - Scope of the governance education progam implemented in 2002.* ASC Publications: Sydney.

Australian Sports Commission. (2002b). *The governance of athletics in Australia: a case study summary.* ASC Publications: Sydney.

Balfour, M. N. (2001). *Parliamentary media briefing.* Internet: <http://www.polity.org.za/html/govdocs/speeches/2001/sp0912a.ht ml> 15 March 2003.

Binns, S., Hamil, S., Holt, M., Michie, J., Oughton, C., Shailer, L. & Wright, K. (2003). *The state of the game - The corporate governance of football clubs 2002.* Football Governance Research Centre: London.

Branston, J.R., Cowling, K. & Sugden, R. (2001). *Research Paper: The public interest in corporate governance.* Internet: <http://www.ub.es/graap/governance.pdf> 14 March 2003.

Brown, A. (2000). European football and the European Union: governance, participation and social cohesion – towards a policy research agenda. *Soccer and Society, 1(2),* 129-150.

Burger, D. (2003). *South Africa Yearbook 2002/03.* 9th Ed. STE Publishers: Johannesburg.

Cadbury Committee Report. (1992). *Report of the Committee on the Financial Aspects of Corporate Governance.* Gee Publishing: London.

Commonwealth Association for Corporate Governance. (1999). CACG Guidelines. Marlborough: Commonwealth Association for Corporate Governance.

DeGroote, M.G. (2000). Facts, myths and monsters: understanding the principles of good governance. *The International Journal of Public Sector Management, 13(2),* 108-124.

Dine, J. (1995). Corporate governance, Cadbury and friendly societies. *Web journal of current legal issues, 1995(1).*

DiPiazza, S.A. (2002). *Speech: Building public trust: the future of corporate reporting.* Internet: <http://accounting.malpractice.com/0005/articlesga-20020617.pdf>. 23 February 2003.

Directorate for Financial, Fiscal and Enterprise Affairs. (1999). *OECD principles of corporate governance.* Paris: Organization for Economic Co-operation and Development.

European Corporate Governance Institute. (No date). Index of codes. Internet: <http://www.ecgi.org/codes/all_codes.htm>. 31 March 2003.

Football Governance Research Centre. (2001). *State of the game: the corporate governance of football clubs.* Internet: <http://www.football-research.org/chap2-Corporate%20Governance.htm>. 15 March 2003.

Football Task Force. (1998a). *Eliminating racism from Football.* London: Football Governance Research Centre.

Football Task Force. (1998b). *Improving facilities for disabled supporters.* London: Football Governance Research Centre.

Football Task Force. (1999). *Football: commercial issues.* London: Football Governance Research Centre.

Foreman, J.A. (2001). *Research: Corporate governance issues in a professional sport.* Victoria: Swinburn University of Technology - School of Business.

Gaved, M. (2001). *Conference Paper: Corporate governance today and its relevance to sport. International Governance in sport.* Internet: <http://www.governance-in-sport.com>. 13 February 2003.

Gerrard, N. (2003). Rethinking regulatory risk: as strategy for the UK and global corporate governance. *Balance Sheet, 11(1),* 37-41.

Governance in Sport Working Group. (2001). *The rules of the Game – Conference report & Conclusions.* Internet: <http://www.governance-in-sport.com>. 14 March 2003.

Gregory, H.J. (No date). *Overview of corporate governance guidelines and codes of best practice in developing and emerging markets.* Internet: <http://www.football-research.org/library.htm>. 30 March 2003.

Hamil, S., Michie, J., Oughton, C. & Shailer, L. (2002). *The state of the game - the corporate governance of Football clubs 2001.* London: Football Governance Research Centre.

Hampel Committee on Corporate Governance. (1998*). Hampel Committee on Corporate Governance - Final Report.* London: Gee Publishing.

Institute of Directors. (2002). *Second King report on corporate governance for South Africa.* Johannesburg: Institute of Directors of Southern Africa.

Institute of Directors. (1994). *King Report on Corporate Governance.* Johannesburg: Institute of Directors of Southern Africa.

International definitions of corporate governance. (2003). Internet: <http://www.ose.no/cg/definisjoner_E.pdf>. 30 March 2003.

Katwala, S. (2000). *Democratizing global sport.* Internet: <http://www.observer.co.uk/Print/0,3858,4421203,00.html>. 8 March 2003.

King, M.E. (2003). *Introduction & background to corporate governance.* Financial Mail. 9 May 2003.

Korac-Kakabadse, N., Kakabadse, A.K. & Kouzmin, A. (2001). Board performance and company performance: any correlations? *Corporate Governance, 1(1),* 24-30.

Malherbe, S. & Segal, N. (2001). *Discussion paper: Corporate governance in South Africa.* Internet: <http://www.oecd.org/dataoecd/9/19/2443999.pdf>. 3 September 2003.

Naidoo, R. (2002). *Corporate Governance: An essential guide for South African Companies.* Cape Town: Double Storey.

News24. (2003). *Boks: Sponsor concerned.* Internet: <http://www.news24.com/News24/Sport/Rugby/0,,2-9-383_1411403,00.html>. 4 September 2003.

Ozanian, M.K. & Decarlo, S. (2003). Does the board have a backbone? *Forbes, 171(10),* 106.

Pretorius, H. (2003). *Eerste kop rol: Regter lei rugby-ondersoek nadat Bok-mediaman bedank.* Beeld. 3 September. pp1.

PricewaterhouseCoopers. (2003). *Corporate Governance Series - Being a Director: duties and responsibilities – King II.* Johannesburg: PricewaterhouseCooper.

Rakhale, V. (2003a). *Bush Bucks set for financial collapse.* Internet: <http://www.businessthroughsport.co.za/index.asp?inc=newsread&article=270>. 17 October 2003.

Rakhale, V. (2003b). *ASA looses major sponsor.* Internet: <http://www.businessthroughsport.co.za/index.asp?inc=newsread&article=317>. 17 October 2003.

Rauter, E. (2001). Good governance = sustainable performance. *The Sport Educator Newsletter, 14(1),* 1.

Reed, H. (2000). Research: *Chapter 10: Corporate governance, board structures and accountability.* London: ESCR Centre for Business Research, University of Cambridge.

Rossouw, D. (2003). *The governance of ethical risk.* Financial Mail. 13 June 2003.

Rossouw, D., de Koker, L., Marx, B. & van der Watt, A. (2003). *Corporate governance & the King II report.* Financial Mail. 16 May 2003.

Ryan, C. (2002). *Sporting bodies urged to practice good governance.* ASC Publications, National Capital Printing: Canberra.

Sankaran G., Volkwein, K.A.E. & Bonsall, D.R. (1999). *HIV/AIDS in sport: impact, issues and challenges.* Aukland: Human Kinetics.

South Africa, 1998a. *South African Sports Commission Act No 109 of 1998.* Pretoria: Government Printer.

South Africa, 1998b. *National Sport and Recreation Act No 110 of 1998.* Pretoria: Government Printer.

South African Sports Commission. (2000). A summary of the contributions of sport to South African society. Pretoria: Sports Information and Science Agency.

Sports Australia. (1999). *The People's Game? 2(2),* 45-47.

Stapledon, G.P. (1998). The Hampel report on Corporate governance. *Companies and Securities Law Journal, 16,* 408-413.

Steele, M. (Summer, 1999). The rise of shareholder intervention. *Management Focus, 12,* 2-6.

Strickwerda, J. (2003). An entrepreneurial model of corporate governance: developing powers to subsidiary boards. *Corporate Governance: International Journal of Business in Society, 3 (2),* 38-57.

Taylor, D.W. (2000). Facts, myths and monsters: understanding the principles of good governance. *The International Journal of Public Sector Management, 13(2),* 109.

The Editor. (2002). *South African boxing dons new gloves.* Internet: <http://www.businessthroughsport.co.za/index.asp?inc=newsread&article=24>. 17 October 2003.

The Editor. (2003). *Banking group ventures into new sponsorship territory.* Internet: http://www.businessthroughsport.co.za/index.asp?inc=newsread&article=127. 17 October 2003.

The Institute of Chartered Accountants in England and Wales. (1999). *Internal Control - Guidance for directors on the combined code.* London: Accountancy books.

Thibault, L. & Harvey, J. (1997). Fostering inter organizational linkages in the Canadian sport delivery system. *Journal of Sport Management, 11,* 45-68.

Van der Berg, C. & Padayachee, A. (2003). *Cronjé cleared – then dumped.* Sunday Times. 31 August 2003. p1.

Van der Berg, C., Munasamy, R. & Schoonmaker, B. (2003). *Straeuli to go.* Sunday Times. 7 September 2003. p1.

Van Heerden, C.H. (2001). Doctoral Thesis: *Factors affecting decision-making in South African sport sponsorships.* Pretoria: Department of Marketing and Communication Management, University of Pretoria.

Ward, H., Borregaard, N. & Kapelus, P. (2002). Corporate citizenship - Revisiting the relationship between business, good governance and sustainable development. *Opinion 1(1),* 1-5. London: International Institute for Environment and Development.

Wilkinson, R. (2003). *Introduction & background to corporate governance.* Financial Mail. 9 May 2003.

THE ETHICS OF CORPORATE GOVERNANCE IN SPORT: THEORY, METHOD, AND OPERATIONALIZATION

Mike McNamee & Scott Fleming

Introduction

On the fields of play, no less than in the boardrooms of international business, unethical practices appear to be flourishing. Recent scandals concerning the Olympic bidding process have, however, shaken the foundations of modern international sport. This is not to suggest that there was ever an age in which such wrongdoing did not exist. It is merely worthy of comment now, more than ever before, because of the globalized nature of much Western sports, the extent to which big businesses are involved in their commodification and development, and the effects of ever-sophisticated methods of investigative journalism. There could never have been a time then, we assert, when a clear framework for the ethics of corporate governance in sport was needed more. This essay maps out an analytical framework in and through which the moral health of sports organizations can be audited on an international basis. To do that, we set out key concepts of (i) ethics; (ii) equity; and (iii) corporate governance. We then develop the model according to three levels of operation: (i) the individual; (ii) the social; and (iii) the political. Finally, we set out a methodology by which professionals and academics can operationalize ethical audits of the governance of sports.

Correspondence to: Dr. M.J. McNamee, Senior Lecturer in Philosophy, Centre for Philosophy, Humanities and Law in Health Care, School of Health Science, University of Wales, Swansea, Singleton Park, Swansea, SA2 8PP, Tel: + 44 1792 602118 Fax: + 44 1792 295769

Ethics

It is perhaps easiest to think of ethics as a form of moral philosophy, or at least the systematic study of moral rules, principles, obligations, agreements, values and norms. This makes the scope of ethics necessarily wide. Under this idea then, we often have to specify the activity or profession that is the object of such systematic study.

In sports, philosophers and social scientists have often been concerned with ethical discussion of individual behaviors such as the in/defensibility of "diving" in football, the nature and levels of respect the players owe to officials, or what rights children have in relation to coaches (Brackenridge, 2001; Tomlinson & Fleming, 1997; McNamee & Parry, 1998). They have also been concerned with those character traits physical educators and sports coaches have attempted to develop (virtues such as courage, fairness, honesty and respect (McNamee, 1995) and those which ought to be challenged and eradicated (vices such as arrogance, dishonesty, racism and sexism (McNamee, 2002; Tamburrini & Tannsjo, 2000; Carrington & McDonald, 2001; Birrell & Cole, 1994).

At a more social level we discuss the un/acceptability of practices such as using performance enhancing supplements (Hoberman, 1992, Houlihan, 1999), the use of genetic engineering (Miah, 2000), intimidating officials, coach harassment (Brackenridge, 2001) and other issues that might be thought of in terms of the culture or moral atmosphere of sports. A proper target here is to understand and develop critical pictures of the ethos's of sports: the relatively shared values and norms of an activity expressed and negotiated on the playing field (Loland & McNamee, 2000).

Finally, we might also consider the political dimension of ethics too. The institutions of sports that are charged with its governance have responsibilities too for the good health of sports in moral and financial matters (Houlihan, 1999). Here, what is required is a vision of corporate ethics, or corporate governance, that is partly general (which could refer to other similar organizations), and partly specific (which depicts the good/benefits of sports).

Equity

In addition to these many aspects of the ethics of sports (and corporate governance in particular) the notion of equity has become particularly prominent in recent times. Equity is an important portion of ethics. It trades essentially on the idea of justice. We often think of justice in the game referring to the ideal of fair play; of observance of the rules and ethos of the game which are designed (in part) to allow an equal opportunity for all concerned to contest the game and win.

Equity itself has many interpretations though it should not simply be confused with equality. Equity addresses the idea of social justice. It concerns the fair distribution of goods, services or other treatment. In sport, as in other areas of life, it is commonly seen as compensatory. Individuals and groups not previously seen to have received fair shares in the lottery of life are compensated by equity policies that seek to redress the situation according to criteria such as need or deservedness.

Equity strategies are typically formed around given populations or groupings related to age, class, disability ethnicity and gender. Increasingly, such equity policies are seen as socially and ethically desirable responses to unethical actions, practices and policies such as exclusivity, homophobia and racism. Equity is seen in contemporary times, therefore, as a crucial component of an ethics strategy by organizations in both public and commercial sectors.

Corporate Governance

Corporate governance is a new term for an old idea. It refers essentially to the idea that an organization has a range of aims or purposes that it must adhere to in ways that are ethically defensible. It entails recognition that some of those aims or purposes must be arranged so that they display integrity within and between them, across the full range of the organization's activities. A central part of corporate governance, then, is the ethical dimension that ranges from hiring practices and financial accountability, to such matters as the cultivation of a loyal workforce.

In her classic text on business ethics, Julia Sternberg (1994) remarks:

'When properly conducted, the ethical audit serves as a key management tool. Through a combination of inspection and interviews, the ethical audit determines the extent to which company decisions at all levels are actually directed at maximizing long-term owner value, and the extent to which they are compatible with distributive justice and ordinary decency.' (p241)

While the context of business to sport is itself a moot point – and one that has been interrogated elsewhere (see, for example, De Sensi & Rosenberg: 1996) there is clearly an issue of substance raised by Sternberg which extends beyond the contexts of mere business and into global sport. While there is a need to be careful to avoid Sternberg's selective focus on decision-making in organizations, there is a much broader canvass to paint when considering the ethics of corporate governance. Specifically, it is necessary to evaluate the entire organizational culture and key decision-making processes. Although the concept of 'long-term owner value' does not translate automatically into the operation of voluntary or state-funded organizations, the idea that an organization's aims and its procedures for achieving them must be open to critique is central. Despite the fact that issues of quality have dominated recent public sector life, in practice, the quality debates have had an essential focus on procedures and have therefore ignored the practices or culture of an organization that define its character. As Sternberg (1994) further remarks:

'An ethical audit actually provides what BS EN ISO 9000 (BS5750) is often - but erroneously - presumed to offer: a standard of quality. BS5750 cannot measure quality, because all it checks is whether a company has applied its procedures systematically; it does not examine the content of those procedures. Unless a procedure is directed at the right end, however, its consistent application simply guarantees consistent wrongness.' (p242)

The Conceptual Model for the Corporate Governance of Sport

In order to carry out the audit thoroughly and effectively, a conceptual model to diagrammatically represent ethics and equity issues within the organization has been developed (see Figure 1). The conceptual model is explicitly concerned with the identification of particular values, and with the main locus of responsibility for each. This conceptual model must then be interrogated through a set of key themes and issues in a series of individual interviews and focus groups of staff of the organization, which is the subject of the audit.

Specifically, the values have to be investigated with reference to the following ideas that formed the parameters of the audit:

- design and delivery of services provided (informed by external market and internal human resource expertise);
- assessment of services delivered;
- evaluation of the effectiveness of the outputs (products and services);
- resource considerations (financial);
- resource considerations (human);
- the experiences of clients/partners; and
- quality assurance of the services provided.

It is important to note that these parameters are used to generate the interviews schedules but do not represent actual questions to be addressed by each focus group or interview.

Explaining and Justifying the Conceptual Framework

Figure 1 represents a potential model of corporate governance. It attempts to lay down, in the form of a conceptual map, an analytical representation of the range of ethical issues in the form of key values. This would operate as a template against which to evaluate an organization's operations from a holistic perspective. The values are listed in alphabetical order, which does not indicate any priorities within the levels. It is, moreover, critical to recognize that the conceptual model does not attempt to describe actual relations nor detail its culture, it is merely an analytical model that sets down key parameters.

In reality, the three levels or dimensions of the conceptual model inter-connect and overlap each other. None works in isolation. Yet to fail to separate out constituent components could render the evaluation subjective and formless.

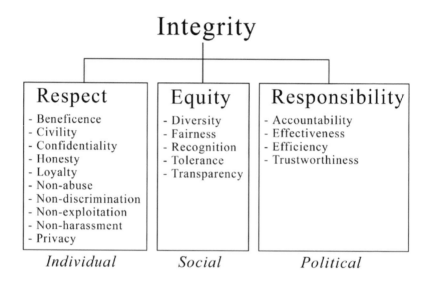

Figure 1. *An ethical approach to the corporate governance of sport* ©.

A primary point of departure is that individuals are responsible for their own conduct and character. Nevertheless, in order to guard against naively individualistic interpretations of the ethical health of the organization's staff, an appreciation is also required of the social and political demands that inform the context of individuals' actions and the policies they seek to implement or operationalize. As McLeod remarks:

> 'The idea that the moral life is largely a matter of carrying out the duties which attach to one's 'station' in society presupposes an unacceptably conformist attitude towards established social arrangements.' (Cited in Solomon, 1993, pp160-1)

The audit must attempt therefore to appreciate the kinds of norms and values that inform daily practice in terms of the ethos of the organization. Only so much insight can be gleaned from a review of formal policies and procedures. Moreover, it is important to bear in mind that a policy or procedure never applies itself. Precisely *how* individuals carry out their duties, *how* they interpret and prioritize procedures, will always be a function of the culture of the organizations.

RESPECT - INDIVIDUAL LEVEL

The first level of the conceptual model identifies values that directly affect the treatment of individuals as employees of the sport organization to be audited. Values that are central here relate to the respect with which individuals are treated. These are essentially negative in keeping with ethical theories based on the nature of rights and duties (see, for example, Davis, 1994). Respect is often captured in the vocabulary of rights and duties. Persons are thought to have certain rights and duties in virtue of their being rationally and morally responsible creatures. To respect people is, in the first place, to be under a duty not to harm them. This is what is captured in the ancient term 'non-malfeasance'. In more modern language this general term is evidenced in particular forms of morally unacceptable behavior such as non-abuse, non-discrimination, non-exploitation or non-harassment.

While other behaviors could be expressed negatively, their more natural expression is in the form of positive values expressed in beneficent action. An altruistic concern for others is often captured in organizational life in terms of the civility offered to colleagues while honesty is critical in all but extreme instances of human interaction. Similarly, and in close relation to recent legislation, moral rights are thought to preserve certain aspects of individuals' lives in relation to that which is properly theirs; this is captured in the values of confidentiality and privacy. In turn, an organization often receives loyalty from members of its workforce (both individually and collectively) in terms of dutiful obligation and allegiance – particularly when there is a sense of shared ownership of the organization's aims, objectives and mission statement. These 'labels' are not necessarily exhaustive but are important types of values that underwrite the ethically desirable treatment of individuals.

This key feature of corporate governance must be twinned with the idea that the organization has proper ends or purposes. One cannot evaluate an organization without a clear sense of those purposes or ends and a consideration of the processes by which they are pursued. In this vein, Edward Johnson (then Chairman of Fidelity Investments) has remarked:

> 'All corporate constituencies – management, stockholders, employees, customers and communities – win from a sound long-term strategy and fair treatment.' (Cited in Sternberg, 1995, p199)

RESPONSIBILITY - POLITICAL LEVEL

The third level of the conceptual model, relating to responsibility, builds upon the idea that an exploration of individuals in social context is incomplete without a proper recognition of the political dimension of their conduct and organizational role as individuals and as an organization. Amelie Rorty has observed that:

> 'Action takes place in a social world. It is, in the end, our social and political relation to others that keeps our virtues in whatever precariously appropriate balance they have.' (1988, p. 325)

Put less prosaically, ethics without politics is like a bicycle without wheels: it isn't going to go anywhere! To fail to address the political dimension of policy and practice would emasculate the ethical audit from the beginning. While the organization's staff, and their client/partner groups expect equity to characterize their treatment of individual staff and their decision-making in the use of public monies (among other things), in state and voluntary sports organizations, and stakeholders in private commercial companies, it is also the case that they properly seek for those organizations to display effectiveness and efficiency and that this is done in a fashion that is accountable. To be ineffective in the use of public or private monies, to fail to evaluate the success of the means employed to achieve its ends may be a matter of irresponsibility, just as the deployment of inefficient means and the selection of inappropriate goals should illicit public opprobrium. Finally, it is clear that such accountability presupposes transparency of operation on the one hand, and the gaining and holding of trust by both employers and partners alike on the other hand.

Respect, Equity and Responsibility

As stated above, the overlap between areas is considerable. In particular, the concerns of equity and responsibility are in constant tensions. At a theoretical level Elster (1992) has remarked:

> 'Political first-order actors (elected politicians) tend, on the whole, to be motivated by efficiency concerns. Being under relentless pressure from innumerable interest groups as well as administrative agencies, they will be reluctant to allocate funds for a particular scarce good unless they can be confident that the funds will be efficiently used. At the highest level, efficiency is measured against the use of the same funds in other sectors. In practice, cross-sector comparisons are difficult, since for financial purposes there is no common coin for health, education and jobs.' (pp. 180-1)

He continues:

> 'Equity does, however, matter, but mainly because politicians are constrained by public opinion in which equity concerns are paramount. Politicians fear allocative scandals; and more scandals arise from the sight of seeing a good withheld from a needy or deserving person than from seeing it allocated to a person who does not use it efficiently. This difference in scandal arousing capacity of inefficiency and inequity are probably due to the fact that costs and damages are dispersed in the former case, and concentrated in the latter.' (p. 181)

It is clear, then, that a more transparent system of political alliances is crucial to the confidence that an organization demands, develops and retains with various agencies as well as the public. Some emphasis must be placed on the divergence of the different strands of operation within an organization, which may well have their own sub-cultures. Auditors must also be conscious of the shifting nature of these relationships at the time of their audit. The audit is, after all, only a 'snap-shot' of the organization at a particular moment in time, albeit informed by the historical development of the organization itself and the biographies of its personnel (cf. Mills, 1958).

Applying the Analytical Framework: Methodology

Each organization has a number of types of 'stakeholders' and the audit should be sufficiently broad in scope to address the views of each of these. Often, depending on the size, complexity and management structure of an organization, these might include: senior managers, middle managers, service / product deliverers, administrative and technical personnel, and cleaning, janitorial and security staff. Amongst these, the culture, ethos and operation of the organization is influenced in a direct relation to institutional hierarchical seniority (see above section on equity). Hence the audit should recognize disproportionate influence within the workforce, and interrogate very closely those who set the ethical climate for the organization. One operational model for the audit is therefore to interview senior managers of the organization individually, to conduct separate focus group meetings with middle managers and service/product deliverers, and to have a wider group discussion with other personnel.

It is crucial, when planning an audit, to develop mutually supportive and collaborative relations with the organization. It is especially important at the agenda-setting stage, that the schedule of issues, policies and practices to be investigated are explored thoroughly before the data collection phase. At this time it is also critical to consider the ethical parameters of the research design and implementation. Protocols for anonymity and confidentiality of the data collected, and the data to be seen by the investigators, must be agreed. Participants must be assured (as far as possible given the size of the organization to be audited) that anonymity of interviewees would be protected. This is especially important when participants may be commenting about individuals within organizations to whom they are institutionally subordinate (for example, 'line-managers'). Moreover, when developing focus groups and wider group discussions it is necessary to establish the 'rules of engagement', which should include a commitment amongst all present to respect the confidentiality of views expressed. The main responsibility of the auditors is to ensure that all identifiers and descriptors about individual focus group participants are removed from the data that are gathered. In reality this is seldom problematic as the details that are revealed in discussion usually serve to illustrate or illuminate a wider point of principle about the organization as a whole.

Equally, to seek to attribute responsibility for good and bad elements of the organizational culture and output would fail to recognize those key persons and posts at which the organization is shaped and driven forward. Throughout an ethics audit it is necessary to attempt to balance between individual and cultural elements. Additionally, auditors must seek to find concrete identifiers (in a variety of possible shapes and sizes) that would provide evidence of the claims made by individuals. To this extent any evaluation will be clearly evidence-based and achieve a level of objectivity required. Consistency amongst multiple data sources serves to strengthen or verify an evaluation about a particular theme (Bryman, 1988). Importantly too, when there are 'causes for concern', these should normally be evidenced from two or more sources. In other words, auditors must not take at 'face value' the subjective assertions of individuals without seeking either policy documentation or corroboration from others persons at different levels of the operation. The fact that a policy exists for, say gender equity, or equality of opportunity in vacancies for employment, does not entail their being observed in practice.

Conclusion
It is clear that a recognition of ethics and equity will move more closely (and self-consciously) to the heart of sports organizations in the 21st century. If an ethics audit of the corporate governance of sport is to be effective it ought to proceed on a rational and relatively objective basis. The conceptual framework that drives the model for an audit presented here is an attempt to capture the often-competing levels of operations within sports organizations from individual to social and political levels. Equally, displaying integrity as an organization will be evidenced in the attempt to reconcile each of these levels and to display the values set out in the framework in both policy and practice. Ethics and equity related concerns are not, and must not be seen to be, issues that are important for only certain departments or persons within any given sports organization. Neither ought it to be perceived as the product of some particular pressure group, but rather the responsibility of all to be actively engaged in the promotion of good corporate governance. In order to develop into a more ethically sound organizational culture, all personnel within sports organizations must make a commitment to improvement in whatever particular forms that takes.

In short, there must be leadership at the Executive level and ownership, at all levels, of the ethics agenda if it is to develop. Additionally, the commitment an organization shows to open itself up to an ethical audit will in itself represent some evidence of corporate governance. This should not, however, be seen as a one-off commitment. It will be necessary to initiate a program that monitors and evaluates the ethics agenda of corporate governance.

Acknowledgement

The research from which this paper is derived is an ethical audit of a national organization involved in the development of sport in Scotland from grass roots to international elite performers. We are grateful to sportscotland for their commissioning of the research and for their support whilst carrying it out. In particular we are grateful to Jon Best, Rose Challies and to Heather Lowden for facilitating the research.

References

Birrell, S. & Cole, C. (Eds). (1994). *Women, sport and culture.* Champaign, Illinois: Human Kinetics.

Brackenridge, C. (2001). *Spoilsports: understanding and preventing sexual exploitation in sport.* London: Routledge.

Bryman, A. (1988). *Quantity and quality in social research.* London: Routledge.

Carrington, B. & McDonald, I. (Eds). (2001). *'Race', sport and British society.* London: Routledge.

Davis, N.A. (1994). 'Contemporary deontology' in P. Singer (Ed.) *A companion to ethics.* Oxford: Blackwell, pp.205-19.

De Sensi, J. & Rosenberg, D. (1996). *Ethics in sport management.* Morganstown: WV: Fitness Information Technology.

Elster, J. (1992). *Local justice: how institutions allocate scarce goods and necessary burdens.* New York: Sage.

Loland, S. (2002). *Fair play: a moral norm system.* London: Routledge.

Hoberman, J. (1992). *Mortal Engines: the science of performance and the dehumanisation of sport.* New York: Free Press.

Houlihan, B. (1999). *Dying to win.* Brussels: Council of Europe.

Loland, S. & McNamee, M.J. (2000). Fair play and the ethos of sports: an eclectic philosophical framework. *Journal of the Philosophy of Sport, XXVII,* pp.63-80.

McNamee, M.J. (1995). Sporting practices, institutions and virtues: a critique and a restatement. *Journal of Philosophy of Sport, XXII,* 61-83.

McNamee, M.J. (2002). Hubris, humility and humiliation; vice and virtue in sporting communities, *Journal of the Philosophy of Sport, XXVIIII*, 1, pp.38-53.

McNamee, M.J. & Parry, J. (Eds) (1998). *Ethics and sport.* London: Routledge.

Mills, C.W. (1959). *The sociological imagination.* Harmondsworth, Middlesex: Pelican.

Miah, A. (2000). The engineered athlete: human rights in the genetic revolution. *Culture, Sport and Society, 3, 3,* pp. 32-52.

Rorty, A. (1988). *Mind in action.* Boston: Beacon Press.

Solomon, R.C. (1993). *Ethics and excellence: cooperation and integrity in business.* Oxford: Oxford University Press.

Sternberg. J. (1994). *Just business: business ethics in action.* London: Warner Books.

Tamburrini, C. & Tannsjo, T. (2000). *Values and sport.* London: Routledge.

Tomlinson, A. & Fleming, S. (Eds.) (1997) *Ethics, sport and leisure: crises and critiques.* Aachen: Meyer & Meyer.

SPORT, CULTURE AND DIFFERENCE: THE SOUTH AFRICAN MODEL(S)

Denise Jones

A Marker of Difference

After the 1994 democratic elections in South Africa (SA), the National Department of Sport and Recreation (DSR) inherited a tripartite system of sport. This consisted of approximately one hundred and fifty sports codes, each of which was governed by bodies representing the different racial groups (African, Colored, White and Indian)[1]. Each had different sporting ideals and the various sporting cultures were racially hierarchical, with Whites the most advantaged and Africans the most disadvantaged.

Sport in South Africa has been a marker of difference. It has reflected the racist attitudes of the early colonizers (Archer and Bouillon, 1982), and been shaped by the institutionalization of racial segregation under the apartheid government and in turn, been shaped by it (Jones, 2001b). It is gendered as male (Hargreaves, JA, 1997; Jones, 1996) and has reflected class differences (Odendaal, 1988; Booth, 1998). This has resulted in the emergence of different sporting cultures. One cannot therefore refer to 'a' South African sporting history. It would be more accurate to refer to 'sport within the history' of South Africa.

---

[1]   For the purposes of this chapter, Black and White will be used as mutually exclusive terms. Black refers to all South Africans who were disenfranchised during the apartheid era. Where it is appropriate to denote a stable category of race or ethnicity, then the terms Indian, African, Coloured (mixed ancestry) or White will be used.

Correspondence to: Prof. Dr. Denise Jones, University of the Western Cape, Private Bag 7535, Belleville, South Africa Tel: +27 21 959 2245 Fax: +27 21 959 3688 Email: djones@uwc.ac.za

In fact, the sporting model (and sporting culture) emerging in post-apartheid South Africa, has been shaped by the unification of these different sporting histories and corresponding sporting cultures.

The aim of this chapter is to outline some of the political issues that have shaped the governance of sport in SA. Unfortunately, the available literature focuses predominantly on sporting males. Where a more critical analysis has been conducted, the focus has been on race as a measure of difference. (Refer, for example, to Brickhill, 1976; Archer and Bouillon, 1982; Booth, 1998; Hendricks, 2001). Few sports theorists have discussed the relationship between sport, women, and gender in SA, with the works of Hargreaves (2000 & 1997) and Jones (2001a and 2001b) being exceptions. Even the National Policy on Sport and Recreation in South Africa (1995) places more emphasis on race than gender, focusing on apartheid-constructed differences based on skin color. It has also equated gender with women, and has limited its reference to 'women' as a target group, listed together with other target groups, such as persons with disabilities and the youth.

In this chapter special attention will be given to the way notions of difference were constructed between the 1940's and 1990's. Due to the scarcity of literature on gender and sport, particular reference will only be made to race, ethnicity and class. For an analysis of gender and sport in the history of South Africa, refer to Jones (2001b).

Role of Sport
Since 1994, there has been a belief in sport as a vehicle for "fostering national unity" in SA. Sport in the country has been recognized as a crucial site in the construction of national identity. The South African National Policy on Sport and Recreation claimed "it is, of course, a matter of record" that the potential of sport to unite the people of SA was obstructed by the apartheid policies. Sport had historically been a signifier of difference, where as now, it was seen as fostering national unity and redressing the (racial) imbalances of the past.

However, some sports theorists, like John Hargreaves (1986) challenge this nation-building role of sport, because it fails to acknowledge differences, contradictions and complexities that create inequalities of power in societies. It also ignores the way power structures work together to maintain differences, which are beneficial to the dominant group in society. This view is supported by South African sports sociologist Hendricks (2001).

In the apartheid era, sports activists had already argued that sport was an integral part of the ideological structures that subjugated people to the evils of apartheid. Erwin, in SACOSPORT (1988), says, "it is apartheid that has inserted politics in sport" and that "segregation and deprival of facilities have been issues of mobilization". This illustrates the link between sport and the power structures of apartheid. SACOSs slogan ' No normal sport in an abnormal society' also highlights this sport-power relationship (Roberts, 1988).

Currently, in SA there is still strong support (especially from politicians) for the nation-building role of sport in the country. There are however, others, like Hendricks (2001) and Jones (2001b), who are in favor of a more critical analysis of the role of sport in post-apartheid SA. Hendricks (2001, 67-68) challenges the belief in the "mystical potential" of sport to "secure positive outcomes for the nation as a whole". Jones (2001b) discusses the way sport in South Africa has shaped identities around notions of difference.

Difference, Identity and the Institutionalization of Sport
BRITISH SPORTING MODEL

By the mid-nineteenth century, Britain had exported its more formal sporting culture and related cultural practices to its colonies (Black & Nauright, 1998). This model of sport reflected British imperialist notions about social hierarchy and public school education. It combined a pseudo-aristocratic ideology of sport with colonialism, which emphasized class, race and gender differences. The construction of identities as sportsmen (not sportswomen) was founded on a belief that these (White not Black) athletes represented the civilized nations (Archer & Bouillon, 1982).

As sport became more institutionalized in SA, it began to reflect these beliefs. The notion of racial separation in SA was determined, firstly, by the British concept of cultural difference, and secondly, on the theories of separation advocated by Afrikaner intellectuals and the Afrikaner nationalist movement (Black & Nauright, 1998). In both instances, race, as a variable emphasizing difference, was the determining factor. A network of social practices in the broader society jointly ensured that power remained in the hands of the dominant group, making access to valued resources, like sport, very difficult. In this way sport became an instrument for promoting the interests of the dominant group(s). In SA this included White, English-speaking males, until 1910, when this was extended to all White males.

THE AFRICAN ELITE

The formalization of sport in the British colonies coincided with both the height of British imperialism as well as with and the transformation of the economy in the British and Boer states in SA after the discovery of gold and diamonds. Of particular significance was the emergence of two identities constructed by African males. While some Africans males were employed as migrant and/or mine workers, there was another group that pursued a different life course. These were referred to as the African elite. By the late 1800s many African males had become British subjects. Formal sport and associated values became an integral part of missionary education for boys (Odendaal, 1988). This was in contrast to girls, where their education focused on femininity and domesticity (Gaitskell, 1988). It was this group of elite males that developed into a new distinct elite class which made demands for Africans in the political system and increasingly gained access to other areas in society as well, such as sport.

Odendaal's (1988) work on these 'Black Victorians' is an illuminating account of the way sport, especially cricket, was used by the Black elite to demonstrate allegiance to the British Crown and to win acceptance in an already racially sensitive society. After South Africa became a Union in 1910, much of this changed. They became disenfranchised and increasingly marginalized, as racial discrimination became institutionalized (Odendaal, 1988, 67). Not surprisingly, the racial segregation had a lasting effect on the structure of sport in SA.

Apartheid Legislation and Sports Governance

There was no specific legislation which forbade mixed sports practices or competitions in SA between the 1920s and 1980s, but the introduction of specific apartheid legislation, segregated South African sport on a formal basis (Ramsamy, 1982, 22-23). This made it made it virtually impossible for any racially mixed sports-related practices to occur without breaking the laws of the country. Table 1 offers an overview of apartheid legislation and its impact on sport in SA.

Sport and politics became more entwined as racial segregation was increasingly entrenched. Various apartheid laws made it impossible for Blacks and Whites to play against each other or to mix socially without special permission. They also denied Blacks access to valued resources needed to make choices and to take advantage of opportunities to the same extent as their White counterparts. Different sporting identities were constructed, based primarily on the color of a person's skin. Eventually, there were more than three hundred laws controlling nearly every aspect of the lives of South Africans (Odendaal, 1995). For example, in 1926 the Liquor Act prevented the integration of ground and club facilities for toilets, refreshments, dancing and seating. The Act forbade Africans from consuming alcoholic drinks with any of the other race groups, except on premises they owned. This effectively prevented people from socializing together after sports matches or at functions. Four further apartheid laws were introduced in the 1950s, which reinforced differences between Blacks and Whites (Jarvie, 1985; Ramsamy, 1982):
1. The population Registrations Act (1950) which determined all sports-related events on the basis of race
2. The Group Areas Act (1950) excluded Black spectators from sports matches and other public entertainment where other racial groups were present, unless a permit had been issued.
3. The Reservation of Separate Amenities Act (1953) permitted owners of property to evict from their premises or exclude members on the basis of race.
4. The Native Law Amendments Act (1957) allowed for the withholding of permission for Africans to attend gatherings and events outside their own native residential area.

Anti-Apartheid, Non-Racial Sports Organizations

From the 1950s, the non-racial sports movement and anti-apartheid activists, within SA and internationally, used sport to transform the country, and influence the development of South African sports. Significant events include: The expulsion of the White South African Table Tennis governing body by the International Table Tennis Federation in 1956. This was the first time that an international federation had demonstrated support for the anti-apartheid movement.

- The establishment of the Committee for the co-ordination of International Relations in Sport by the non-racial sports bodies in South Africa in 1956. This was the first attempt by international sports bodies to co-ordinate the registration of players to non-racial sports organizations in South Africa.
- The apartheid government's official statement against racially mixed sport in 1956. This was the state's first official standpoint on segregation in South African sport
- The establishment of the South African Sports Association (SASA) in 1958. This was the first non-racial organization to be formed by sports activists who were challenging apartheid in South African sport.

The establishment of SASA highlighted differences in a particular way. Firstly, its creation marked the acceptance of non-racial sport as a key principle in the struggle against apartheid. It also signified a shift from viewing sport in terms of Black and White to defining it in terms of a 'dominant sporting culture' (to which the majority of Whites sports persons were affiliated) and those (predominantly Black) sports persons who rejected apartheid.

Secondly, SASA provided a common identity for sports activists. It offered them an opportunity to support the broader struggle against apartheid (Brickhill, 1976). SASA and the African National Congress (ANC) worked together in their attempts to create an international awareness of the oppression of apartheid (Roberts, 1988).

Thirdly, the formation of SASA was an attempt to deal with apartheid at a structural level. The difficulties SASA encountered at the more practical level were partly attributed to the success of the apartheid government in dividing Blacks into distinct racial categories as Africans, Indians and Coloreds.

In 1962, the South African Non-Racial Olympic Committee (SANROC) replaced SASA. This heralded a different approach in the anti-apartheid struggle in the sporting context. SANROC increasingly challenged the racial basis on which South African sports were organized in the Black communities (Jarvie, 1985). Its task was to mobilize international solidarity and seek recognition for Black sports persons, while upholding non-racial principles (Roberts, 1988).

In 1973, the South African Council on Sport (SACOS) was established. It affected the direction of the non-racial sports movement both locally and internationally, by adopting a more aggressive approach to challenging apartheid and promoting non-racial sport that was illustrated by:

- Refusing to separate sporting demands from broader demands for social change.
- Adopting a policy of no negotiations.
- Declaring solidarity among non-racial sports organizations until the symbols of apartheid had been removed not only from sport but from South African society.
- Instituting a self-imposed international sports moratorium.

Table 1. *Sports Governance in South Africa (1949-1998).*

YEAR	EVENT	SIGNIFICANCE FOR SPORT
1948	Nationalist Party comes to power in South Africa	Official apartheid policy separates Blacks and Whites at both the institutional level and the level of the body
1949	Prohibition of Mixed Marriages Act	Emphasized differences and combined with other legislation to shape the construction of identity as sportswomen and sportsmen
1950	Populations Registrations Act	Determined sporting categories and the organization of all sports events and training on the basis of race
1950	Group Areas Act	Excluded Black spectators from sports matches where Whites were present unless a permit was obtained
1956	South African (White) Table Tennis governing body expelled by the International Table Tennis Federation	Recognition was given to the non-racial Table Tennis Board which represented Black sportswomen and sportsmen in SA
1956	Committee for the coordination of International Relations in SA Sport established by the non-racial sports organizations	The domain of sport and the issue of non-racial sport was formally incorporated into the political arena of the state
1956	The apartheid government's first official statement on racially mixed sport	No inter-racial sports competition would be tolerated in SA, including international touring teams
1957	Native Law Amendments Act	Permission could be withheld from Africans wanting to attend events outside their designated residential areas
1958	The South African Sports Association (SASA) was establishment	Goals of non-racial sports organizations were made more visible and their resistance to apartheid in sport more coordinated.
1959	Cancellation of (male) football match between Brazil and a White South African team and cancellation of (male) cricket tour by a West Indian team against Black South Africans	These were indicators of SASAs success against apartheid in sport
1961	SA expelled from the Commonwealth Games	This was a major international action against apartheid in sport
1962	The South African Non-Racial Olympic Committee (SANROC) replaced SASA	A different approach was adopted in challenging the apartheid government's policies which involved the mobilization of international solidarity

Table 1 cont...

1964	SA was excluded from the Tokyo Olympic Games	This represented SANROCs first major international strike against apartheid in sport
1967	The second policy related to sport was announced	The policy allowed for the selection of any Black sportsperson on merit but no racially mixed sports would be practiced locally. Blacks and Whites would separately administer their sports
1968	SA is expelled from the Mexico Olympics	South Africa's sporting future became a cause of concern
1969	SA held it's own Mini-Olympic Games for Whites	South Africa's isolation was highlighted. The South African government felt a need to compensate the White athletes
1971	SA unveils a multi-national sports policy	It was an indication of the apartheid government's willingness to change its policy towards racially mixed sport
1973	The South African Council on Sport (SACOS is established	SACOS adopted an approach which refused to separate sporting demands for social change
1980	The Human Sciences Research Council (HSRC) was commissioned by the South African Government to investigate the nature of sport in SA	HSRC recommended that a SA sports council be established as a corporate body. It proposed a less fragmented sports structure. Discrepancies in the allocation of facilities were highlighted. It advocated that apartheid legislation be amended
1982	The Conservative Party was formed	The apartheid government had scope to pursue its efforts to depoliticize sport in SA
1988	The National Olympic Sports Congress (NOSC) is established	Spot in SA entered a new era as the NOSC became the new leaders of the non-racial sports movement as unity-in-spot talks proceeded
1994	The Department of Sport and Recreation is restructured	A role for sport had been identified in the reconstruction and transformation of a new democratic SA
1998	The South African Sports Commission Bill and the National Sport and Recreation Bill are passed	The sport and recreation minister and his department were given more power to initiate and enforce change in South Africa sport

Apartheid and International Sport Boycotts

In the 1960s the apartheid government was forced to alter its attitude towards racially integrated sport, because of the tension between upholding its previous statements opposing racially mixed sport and the increasing international pressure to dismantle apartheid. Its earlier attempts at segregated sports governance and the implications thereof, are illustrated by the following:

In 1961 the International Olympic Committee (IOC) issued an ultimatum to the South African Olympic Games Association (SAOGA) to change the apartheid situation as it related to sport, by the October 1963 session of the IOC, or SA would be expelled from the Olympic Movement. SAOGAs response referred to biology and science to justify the exclusion or inclusion of Black sports persons:

- Firstly, the SAOGA re-iterated its emphasis on racial differences by claiming that segregation within sporting system in SA would continue because this was part of government policy.
- Secondly, it conceded that Blacks would be selected on merit for the Olympic team, providing there was no direct competition with Whites. In this eventuality, the SAOGA had prepared an elaborate method of selection for differentiating between sports persons from racially different groups.

The IOC rejected the proposal and consequently SA was excluded from the Tokyo Olympic Games in 1964. In 1967, a year before the Mexico Olympics, Prime Minister Vorster announced a second policy related to sport. It made a distinction between sports participation at the international level and at the local level. Black sports persons could represent their country, but on their return to the country, not only would their "otherness" to Whites continue to significantly impact on their life circumstances, but their differences in relation to each other as African, Indian or Colored sports persons would continue to be effective.

The policy reaffirmed that no racially mixed sports would be practiced locally.   In addition, Blacks and Whites would administer their sports separately.   This seemingly gave more autonomy to Black sports organizations, but in effect further institutionalized racial segregation.   A warning was issued to other countries that SA would not compromise on the matter of mixed-race teams (Brickhill, 1976: 21-22).   This did not appease the IOC or delegates to a United Nations Human Rights Conference in 1968. SA was therefore excluded from the 1968 Olympics as well. Refer to Thoma and Chalip (1996:163-164) for a discussion on the use of the sport's boycott as political sanctions against SA.

Multi-National (Sports) Policy
From the early 1970s, South Africa's international sporting relations were not only seriously threatened, but were also severely transformed by the non-racial sports campaign (Jarvie, 1985). Fearing a complete boycott of South African sport, there were requests to government from White sports persons and administrators within the country to permit various degrees of racial integration. In 1971 a new sports policy was unveiled and was referred to as a multi-national sports policy. It was concessionary in its attitude to racially mixed sport.

This multi-national policy raised a range of issues that are linked to the three key principles on which it was founded:
- To create separate Indian, Colored, and African autonomous sporting associations.
- To finance and promote the emergence of a small Black sporting elite.
- To force this Black elite to support the status quo and official apartheid policies.

This did little to foster a national sports identity. Instead:
- It promoted alternative sporting cultures, each of which was shaped by access to valued resources.
- It meant that within SA, the different racial groups were permitted to compete against each other as four separate nations. However, at club or provincial levels, mixed or multi-racial sport was still not permitted.
- It did not permit Blacks to compete against international players unless it was a major international event (Roberts, 1988).

- It cultivated a diverse South African sports system which was racially hierarchical with African sports persons the most disadvantaged because they did not possess any form of control over sporting facilities. They were also dependent on White organizations and municipalities for funding (Brickhill, 1976).

In order to give the impression internationally that a major policy shift had taken place, sport in SA was marketed as being multi-national, even multi-racial. However, at the grass roots level, economic and political factors prevented this from taking place. The unequal distribution of resources with respect to facilities, training, and sponsorship, resulted in gross inequalities in circumstance, which continued to be reflected in unequal access and opportunity in the dominant (White) sports system. In reality, differences were emphasized and apartheid was perpetuated, as each race group was allowed to develop its own separate sporting practices on condition that the White administered sports bodies remained in overall control and continued to determine the nature of sporting practices in SA.

African sports persons were still governed by Pass Laws that restricted their movements and prevented them from traveling freely to play matches or go on tours. In addition, while non-racial sports officials and sports persons continually faced intimidation by security forces and prosecution (Hain, 1982), those Black sports officials who had been co-opted to the White sports bodies were able to travel freely, with costs sometimes being covered by the White sports organizations (Grundlingh, 1995). By the late 1970s, integrated clubs and integrated sport in South Africa constituted less than one per cent of total sports activities in the country.

The struggle and tension between different sporting cultures in South Africa increased. This complex situation was represented by a unique tri-partite sporting structure (Jarvie, 1985, 48), which comprised:
- The dominant (White) government-controlled sports.
- The non-racial sports movement co-ordinated and driven during the 1950s to 1980s by SASA, SANROC, SACOS and NSC, respectively.
- A group of Black sports people who confined membership of their sports bodies to Africans, Asians and Colored.

In addition, Black sports federations affiliated to White sporting federations. The multi-national sports policy was consequently rejected (Jarvie, 1985). It was at this stage that SACOS adopted the slogan "no normal sport in an abnormal society" (Roberts, 1988).

Depoliticizing South African Sport

In the 1980s the apartheid government made various efforts to grant more autonomy to the sports codes themselves, as a way of depoliticizing South African sport. This policy shift was the combined result of resistance from within the country and international pressure in the form of:

- Increasing international sporting isolation.
- The adoption of the Gleneagles Agreement.
- Increasing resistance to international sports tours.

Strategies were aimed at:

- Making political concessions to deal with the sports boycott.
- Attracting international sportspeople.
- Enticing affiliates from African sports structures and players from the townships.

The removal of petty-apartheid legislation did little to bring about real changes. The years of institutionalized apartheid had created structural obstacles that were often too enormous to allow advantage to be made of these new opportunities. For example:

- Although Blacks were legally able to participate in mixed sport at previously designated White sports clubs, little was done to alter the inequalities prevalent in the social, economic and political structures of South African society.
- Scarcity of transport and the distances between clubs and areas historically allocated to Blacks made regular attendance of practices and matches difficult.
- A lack of access to adequate coaching resources and facilities impacted negatively on performances.

Meanwhile, changes were occurring in the nature of the anti-apartheid struggle. This inevitably led to changes within the non -racial sports movement itself. SACOS made valiant efforts to broaden it's affiliate-base, while simultaneously upholding the belief that an *abnormal society* could not foster normal development in sport. While the vision of SACOS did represent the aspirations of the majority of disenfranchised South Africans, it was unfortunately not mass-based (Roberts, 1988). SACOS maintained its hard-line approach to the sports moratorium and policy on double standards, forbidding any of its members to participate in any sports code that practiced or condoned racialism and multi-nationalism (SACOSPORT, 1988).

In 1988, sport in the country had entered a new era, as SACOS and the National Sports Olympic Congress (NOSC) vied for the powerful status of being accepted by the population as the leaders of the non-racial sports movement in the country (Jurgens, 2000). Consequently, the late 1980s saw the emergence of the National Sports Congress, which eventually became known as the NSC.

Governance of Sport in Post-Apartheid South Africa
SPORTS STRUCTURES
Prior to the democratic elections in SA in 1994, the objectives and operations of the national Department of Sport is outlined in Table 1. When the new post-apartheid sports culture emerged, it included:
- The restructuring of the DSR.
- The formulation of sports policies.
- The establishment of sports structures at national, provincial and regional levels.

In addition, the DSR achieved status as an independent department. This signified the importance attributed to sport in the reconstruction and transformation of the new SA. By mid 1990, a national White paper on Sport and Recreation was circulated and soon after became the official policy on sport and recreation for SA (National Policy on Sport and Recreation, 1995). In 1996, various structures for Women and Sport were also established in each of the seven provinces.

Other additional structures (macro-structures) were established for the advancement of sport, including:
- The National Sports Council (NSC) as the umbrella body for South African sport
- The South African National Recreation Council (SANREC) as the umbrella body for recreation
- The National Olympic Committee of South Africa (NOCSA)
- Women and Sport South Africa (WASSA)

National and provincial sport and recreation forums and councils, together with structures for school and university sports, now support the macro sports structures. For example:
- The United School Sports Union of South Africa (USSASA)
- The South African Students Union (SASU)
- The Sport Information and Science Agency (SISA)
- The Sports Science Institute (SSI)
- The Western Cape Sports Academy (WECSA)
- Sports Coaches' Outreach (SCORE). This is a non-governmental organization providing sports opportunities for township children.

At a legislative level, two sports-related bills were passed in 1998. This gave the Sport and Recreation Minister and his Department more power to initiate and enforce change, rather than rely on a culture of goodwill (Hendricks, 2000). The bills are the South African Sports Commission Bill and the National Sport and Recreation Bill

Another key development was the establishment of the South African Sports Commission (SASC) in 1999 (Gilpin, 1999, 184). The Chief Executive Officer of the SASC is accountable to the Minister of Sport and Recreation who has significantly been able to maintain the Department of Sport and Recreation as his power base, despite the formation of the Sports Commission.

ADDRESSING INEQUALITIES

Despite the establishment of Women and Sport South Africa (WASSA), the new DSR has adopted a radical approach in transforming the racial inequalities, but a liberal approach in addressing gender inequalities. Consequently, issues around race have periodically become a national problem, while gender inequalities seem to remain a problem for the women's structures to resolve.   In 1997 the NSC resolved to undertake a unity audit on racial imbalances in sports.   A year later, the new government declared its intention to implement legislation, which would mandate that the selection of national sports teams should include Black players (Survey 1999/2000).

Merit remains the only criteria for the selection of national teams. To this end, some national federations have signed performance agreements with the Minister of Sport in which they have undertaken to reach specific representivity targets, within specified timeframes (Hendricks, 2002). Similar aggressive strategies have not been adopted in addressing the gender inequalities in sport.

Following the Sydney Olympics in 2000, a Ministerial Task Team (MTT) was established to investigate the status of high performance sport in SA. This was motivated by a desire to rationalize the structures and services available to all athletes. In addition, the MTT focused on equity issues, early talent identification, rationalization of the operation of sports organizations at both government and non-governmental levels, as well as the need to introduce recreational sport, especially at school level (Burchell, 2002). The MTT report has subsequently been accepted by the South African Government.

The immediate consequences have been: (i) the repeal of the Sports Commissions Act, (ii) agreement in principle for the establishment of a National Academy of Sport, and (iii) the signing of a co-operation agreement between seven macro-organizations[1] to rationalize and realign the major sports organizations in South Africa around (a) managing multi-purpose teams, (b) creating a data base, and (c) emerging sports operations.

This process will be managed by the MTT steering committee which has been given a mandate to: (a) form a new non-governmental organization to co-ordinate 'high performance sport', and (b) realign the structure of sport in South Africa by creating a new fully-fledged government department (Burchell, 2004) which will replace the current National Department called 'Sport and Recreation South Africa'. Its 'business ' will be the governance of mass sports participation and addressing equity issues in sport. After the recent 2004 government elections, Balfour was replaced by Stofile as the new Minister of Sport and Recreation.

Conclusion

The focus of this chapter was on 'cultural differences' and sport. To this end, the South African model was selected as a way of illustrating how 'culture and difference' can shape sporting history with an emphasis on political issues around sport leadership in South Africa. More specifically, the role of sport as a marker of difference was outlined. The influence of the British model of sport and the way apartheid legislation impacted on the development of South African sport was explained. The role of the non-racial sporting bodies and the international sport boycotts during the apartheid era were discussed. A table illustrating sports governance in South Africa from 1949-1998 was presented. The attempts by the apartheid government to depoliticize South African sport were described. Finally, an overview of the governance of sport in post-apartheid South Africa was offered up to and preceding the Olympic Games in Greece in 2004.

---

[1] The seven macro-organizations are (1) The South African Commonwealth Games Association, (2)The United School Sports Union South Africa, (3) The National Olympic Committee of South Africa, (4) The South African Students Sports Association, (5) Disability Sport South Africa, (6) Sports Commission (7) Sport and Recreation South Africa

References

Archer, R. & Bouillon, A. (1982). *The Sporting Game*. London: Zed Press.

Black, D.R & Nauright, J. (1998). *Rugby and the South African Nation: Sport, Cultures, Politics and Power in the Old and New South Africa*. Manchester: Manchester University Press.

Booth, D.G. (1998). *The Race Game: Sport and Politics in South Africa*. London: Frank Cass.

Brickhill, J. (1976). *Race against Race: South Africa's Multinational Sport Fraud*. London: International Defence and Aid Fund.

Burchell, A. (2002). South African Sports Commissioner. Telephonic interview, Cape Town: South Africa, 20th June.

Burchell, A (2004) General Manager, Disability Sport South Africa. Telephonic Interview, Cape Town, South Africa. 5th July.

Gaitskell, D. (1988). Race, Gender and Imperialism: A Century of Black Girls' Education in South Africa. In J.A. Mangan (Ed.) *Benefits Bestowed*, Chapter 8.

Gilpin, T. (1999). Match Makers: A Case for South African Sport. Cape Town: TED Gilpin.

Grundlingh, A. (1995). Playing for Power. In A. Grundlingh, A. Odendaal and B. Spies (Eds) *Beyond the Tryline: Rugby and South African Society*. Johannesburg: Ravan Press, pp.106-131.

Hain, P. (1982). The Politics of Sport Apartheid. In J.A. Hargreaves (Ed) *Sport, Culture and Ideology*. London: Routledge & Kegan Paul.

Hargreaves, J. (1986). *Sport, Power and Culture.* Oxford: Polity Press.

Hargreaves, J.A. (1997). Women's Sport, Development, and Cultural Diversity: The South African Experience. *Women's Studies International Forum*, 20(2), pp.191-209.

Hargreaves, J. (2000). Race, Politics and Gender: Women's Struggles for Sport in South Africa. (Chapter 2). In *Heroines of sport: The politics of difference and identity*. London: Routledge, pp.14-45.

Hendricks, D.J. (2000). Acting Director General Department of Sport and Recreation. Telephonic interview, January.

Hendricks, D. (2001a). Nation-Building and the Business of Sport. *Perspectives-The Multidisciplinary Series of Physical Education and Sport Science*, 3, pp.65-76.

Hendricks, D.J. (2001b). Head - Department of Sport and Recreation. E-mail correspondence, December.

Jarvie, G. (1985). *The political economy of white sporting practice in Class, race and Sport in South Africa's Political Economy* (Chapter 3). London: Routledge.

Jones, D.E.M. (1996). The Emergence of a Non-Alternative Physical Education for females in South Africa, Sport as Symbol, Symbols in Sport: *International Society for the History of Physical Education and Sport*: ISHPES-studies Series, vol., 4.

Jones, D.E.M. (2001a). In Pursuit of Empowerment: Sensei Nellie Kleinsmidt, Race and Gender Challenges in South Africa. In J.A. Mangan & F. Hong (Eds) Special Issue freeing The Female Body Inspirational Icons. *The International Journal of the History of Sport*, 18(1), pp.219-236.

Jones, D.E.M. (2001b). 'Gender, Sport and Power: The Construction of Identities as Sportswomen in South Africa. Unpublished Doctoral Dissertation, Utrecht University, Netherlands.

Jurgens, D.J. (2000). Personal interview. Newlands, Cape Town: South Africa.

Odendaal, A. (1995). The Thing that is not Round. In A Grundlingh, A. Odendaal & B. Spies (Eds) *Beyond the Tryline* (Chapter 2).

Odendaal, A. (1988). South Africa's Black Victorians: Sport and Society in South Africa in the Nineteenth Century in J.A. Mangan (Ed) *Pleasure, Profit, Proselytism: British Culture and Sport at Home and Abroad 1700-1914*. London: Frank Cass, pp.193-214.

Ramsamy, S. (1982). *Apartheid: The Real Hurdle*. London: International Defence and Aid Fund for Southern Africa.

Roberts, C. (1988). *SACOS 1973-1988: 15 Years of Sports Resistance*. Cape Town: Township Publishing.

SACOSPORT FESTIVAL (1988). A commemorative Volume. Cape Town: Buchu Books.

South Africa Survey 1999/2000. Millennium edition. *South African Institute of Race Relations.* Johannesburg: South Africa.

Thoma, J.E. & Chalip, L. (1996*). Sport Governance in the Global Community.* Morgantown, WVA: Fitness Information Technology.

White Paper on Sport and Recreation (1995). National Department of Sport and Recreation, Pretoria: South Africa.

Additional Reading

Guelke, A. (1986). The Politicization of South African Sport. In L. Allison (Ed) *The Politics of Sport*. Manchester: Manchester University Press, pp.151-170.

Hargreaves, J.A. and Jones, D. (2001). 'South Africa'. In K. Christensen; A. Guttmann & G. Pfister (Eds) *International Encyclopaedia of Women and Sports*. New York: Macmillan Library, pp.395-402.

Jarvie, G. (1992). Sport, Power and Dependency in Southern Africa. In E. Dunning & C. Rojek (Eds) *Sport and Leisure in the Civilising Process: Critique and Counter-Critique* (Chapter 8). Toronto: University of Toronto Press.

Nauright, J. (1997). *Sport, Cultures and Identities in South Africa*. London: Leicester University Press.

van der Merwe, F.J.G . (1997). *Sport History: A Textbook for South African Students*. Stellenbosch: F.J.G. Publications.

Black, D.R and Nauright, J. (1998). *Rugby and the South African Nation: Sport, Cultures, Politics and Power in the Old and New South Africa*. Manchester: Manchester University Press.

de Broil, C. (1970). *South Africa: Racism in Sport*. London: International Defence and Aid Fund.

Kidd, B. (1991). From Quarantine to Cure: The New Phase of Struggle against Apartheid Sport. *Sociology of Sport Journal*, 8, pp.33-46

Krotee, M.L. (1988). Apartheid and Sport: South Africa revisited in *Sociology of Sport Journal*, 5: 125-135.

National Strategy of Women and Sport South Africa (1997). National Department of Sport and Recreation: Pretoria, South Africa.

Policy on Affirmative Action (1999). National Sports Council: Pretoria, South Africa.

BASIC PERSPECTIVES OF PARLIAMENTARY LAW AND PROCEDURES

Darlene Kluka and Lionel Gilbert

For over fifty years, parliamentary rules of order have continued to be a most useful tool for thousands of professionals involved in sport governance. In order to provide guidelines for procedures to conduct the business of any organization, *Robert's Rules of Order* has been found to be the most commonly adhered to because of its clarity and ease of use (Hums & McaLean, 2004). Parliamentary procedure can facilitate the conduct of business meetings and provide leaders with a structure that sets a framework for cooperation and civility. Several important basic perspectives will be presented in this chapter to provide basic parliamentary rules of order and procedures for future use.

FUNDAMENTAL TENETS

Fundamental tenets of parliamentary procedure for governance were originally designed to implement the concepts of equality, specifically involving rights, obligations, and privileges. The most fundamental of these tenets involve both decision and protection. The majority in an organization has the right to make decisions while the minority in the organization must be protected. With this as a backdrop, the following tenets delineate a functional framework:

Correspondence to: Darlene A. Kluka, Ph. D., Grambling State University of Louisiana, Dept. of Kinesiology, Sport and Leisure Studies, P.O. 1193, Grambling, Louisiana, 71245 USA Tel: + 1 318 274 2602, Fax: : +1 318 274 6053, Email: eyesport@aol.com

1. In order to conduct a successful meeting, the chair and members must plan in advance.
2. Five types of knowledge are important when participating in a meeting:
   a. Content knowledge – brokering information about the topics involved
   b. Parliamentary rules of order knowledge – brokering information about legitimate procedures used in the conductance of business
   c. Persuasive knowledge – the ability to influence others' decisions
   d. Decision making knowledge –brokering of information about making decisions
   e. Group dynamics knowledge – brokering of information about human social-emotional interactions
3. The purpose of the meeting and each agenda item needs to be clear to members:
   a. To provide information and ideas to the group
   b. To inform members before action is taken
   c. To provide new ideas
   d. To facilitate decision making by the group
   e. To provide recommendations for consideration and action by the group
4. In order to conduct official business at a meeting, a quorum must be present. This ensures that decisions voted upon represented the majority of those eligible to conduct business on behalf of the organization.
   a. If a vote is taken when there is no quorum, the vote is void;
   b. The person presiding is responsible for determining whether a quorum exists; it is the responsibility of those present to state an absence of a quorum should it occur once the meeting begins.
5. An agenda is an order of business to be conducted at the meeting. It is helpful when the agenda is published in advance of the meeting. (See Appendix A for a sample agenda)
6. The chair recognizes members to speak. No one can speak twice on the same motion unless all others have been provided with the opportunity to speak once.

7. One item of business can be presented at a time. An agenda assists the presiding person with the order of business.

Committees

A committee, referred to in parliamentary law, is a group of one or more elected or appointed people, who consider, look into, or take action on topics of interest to the committee. To function effectively and efficiently, a committee must have (a) a list of members; (b) legitimate power and duties; (c) a copy of the motion that was referred to them;(d) instructions, including what their task is and action to be taken; (e) copies of papers that are related to the topic given; (f) copies of policies, decisions, or rules that might impact or limit the committee in its ability to resolve the task; and (g) timeline for completion of the task and the type of report that is to be submitted.

Committee reports should include the following:

1. What task the committee was charged with
2. What methods were used by the committee to complete the task
3. Summary of work done, including findings and conclusions. For long reports, an executive summary is included at the beginning of the report
4. Specific recommendations, including rationale
5. Committee member names

When organizing and completing the report, two goals should be kept in mind. First, the committee's report should be accepted by the governing body that requested the report. Second, the report should provide recommendations that could be feasibly implemented.

Motions

Before discussion and a vote can be taken on one item of business at a time, a motion (a proposal formally made in a meeting) and a second (a formal endorsement of a motion by a voting member) must be presented. Once a motion and a second are presented, debate on the motion can occur. Members take turns, speaking one person at a time, to discuss the motion. The person presiding (chair) remains impartial in the debate, but determines which person speaks. Generally, one person will speak in favor of the motion, alternating with one person who will speak against the motion.

Any vote that precludes the rights of the minority or members who are absent requires 2/3 of those present to vote in favor for a motion to be accepted. Once the vote is taken, members can expect that the action is adopted and will be carried out. Members *may* reconsider, rescind, or change the motion by making an amendment.

The right to debate the motion first belongs to the person who presented the motion. If someone else begins speaking to the motion, the chair is responsible for asking whether the maker would like to speak to it first.

When debating a motion, comments made must be relevant and specific to the motion. For example, if the motion involves the adoption of a document involving conflict of interest for board members, it would not be germane to comment on a vote for who the next president of the organization might be.

During debate, members may not emotionalize statements. For example, questioning or attacking another member's motives is inappropriate. The member can, however, question the implications or consequences of the motion by providing strong evidence to the contrary of statements made by others.

Members make all statements (through the chair) providing support for the motion or statements contrary to the motion. Addressing other members directly is inappropriate; asking questions for clarity, however, is permissible. Questioning for clarity is referred to as a *point of information.*

Once a motion is voted upon, a member may not speak against it at a later time unless there is first a motion to reconsider, rescind, or amend it. The member making a specific motion cannot speak against the motion, but *can* vote against it.

Any member, including the chair, can use the technique of *point of order* to temporarily cease debate on a motion when the situation becomes disorderly. Point of order can be used to clarify the order of procedures, assist with unruliness of behavior, or other relevant matters to civility.

Language used

When making a motion, the following language is used:

Member 1: Madam President,

Chair: (Nod of head) (The chair also recommends that the maker of the motion complete a motion form so that the motion is in print and includes the signature of the motion maker and the second.)

Member 1: I move that the Board of Directors adopt the *Codes of Behavior* as presented.

Member 2: Second

Chair: It is moved and seconded that the Board of Directors adopt the *Codes of Behavior* as presented. Is there any discussion?

Member 1: Madam President, discussion....

Member 3: (If there is an amendment to the main motion) Madam President,

Chair: (Nod of head)

Member 3: I move to amend the motion by inserting the words "...by the Task Force" after "...as presented."

Member 4: Second

Chair: It is moved and seconded to amend the motion to insert after the words 'by the Task force' after *'presented'*.

When taking the vote:

Chair: The question is on the adoption of the proposed amendment to insert 'by the Task Force' after the word 'presented'. If the amendment is adopted, the motion would read, it is moved and seconded that the Board of Directors adopt the *Codes of Behavior* as presented by the Task Force. All those in favor of the amendment, say "aye". Those opposed, say "no". Abstentions?

Members then cast their votes.

- If the amendment is passed, that is, a majority vote in favor of the amendment:

Chair: The amendment is carried, and 'by the Task Force' will be inserted after the word 'presented'. The question is on the motion as amended that the Board of Directors adopts the *Codes of Behavior* as presented by the Task Force. Is there any discussion?

- If the amendment is not passed:

Chair: The amendment is lost. We will not insert and 'by the Task Force' after the word 'presented'. Is there any further discussion on the Board of Directors adopting the *Codes of Behavior* as presented?

The following table provides a summary of frequently used motions to facilitate work of the organization.

Table 1. *Frequently used motions.*

Desired Action	Action
Present something for action	Main motion; resolution
Improve a motion before the group	Amend
Confine debate	Limit or extend debate; call for question
Gain information on a motion before the group	Request for information; question of privilege; request to ask member a question
Delay a vote	Refer to committee; postpone; postpone indefinitely (which effectively kills the motion)
Question the chair	Point of order; appeal decision of the chair
Get rid of a motion before the group	Withdraw the motion; postpone indefinitely

Voting

Voting is a basic requirement for approval of an action by the organization. There are three appropriate responses that members may use when voting: Yes (yea); no (nay); or I abstain. Several methods of voting can be used to assist in the conductance of business at meetings. They include: *Voice vote*, which describes casting of a vote by voice and is the most frequently used method. This is particularly popular if no more than a simple majority vote is needed; *Rising vote* refers to a voice vote when there is indefinite results, particularly those votes requiring 2/3 majority; *Show of hands* is used as an alternative to a voice vote and is conducted by raising of hands. A member can request a show of hands by asking the chair for a call for a division of the house (The member would ask, 'Madam Chair, I call for a division of the house').

A *ballot vote* is conducted when secrecy of individual votes is desired. In some cases, ballot vote is mandated by bylaws of a constitution. Ballot votes are preferred when action is proposed against a member of the organization; and a *Roll call* vote may be used when each member's vote must be recorded on a particular issue so that constituents can hold the member accountable.

A simple majority vote describes where more than half of those eligible to vote cast a vote in favor of a motion.

Minutes

Minutes serve as the official record of proceedings of a meeting of an organization. These include committee meetings, commission meetings, board meetings, and general assembly meetings. The official record includes action taken at the meeting, not only what was discussed at the meeting. A combination of actions taken and discussion points make a more precise record of the meeting environment. A Secretary is generally responsible for preparation of the minutes, whereas in some groups, a staff member is designated to perform this function. In other cases, the chair of the group prepares the minutes. Draft minutes, once completed, are first submitted to the group for approval. As property of the organization, the group must formally approve the draft minutes. The chair asks the group to approve the minutes by stating, "...Are there any additions or corrections to the minutes as read? If not, the minutes are approved as presented." If there are corrections to the minutes, then the Secretary or designee notes the corrections, and the minutes are then approved as corrected.

Generally, the minutes should include the following details:
- name of the group
- date, time, and place of the meeting
- the name of the chair and Secretary for the meeting
- a record of those who were in attendance
- and whether or not the minutes from the previous meeting were approved (as read or as corrected).

The minutes also include topics, by paragraph, discussed during the meeting. Each paragraph should contain motions made and actions taken by the group. The Secretary or recorder signs the minutes at the end.

CONCLUSION

The rules used to determine the conductance of organizations involved in the governance of sport and sport-related enterprises can provide leaders with a structure that sets a framework for cooperation and civility. Governing bodies at the local, national, regional, and international levels have roles and responsibilities that share common characteristics that can benefit from the use of Parliamentary Law and Procedures. The process by which sport and sport-related enterprises are governed should be placed in print so that people new to governance concepts can be facilitated and encouraged.

Appendix

Sample agenda for organizational meetings, following parliamentary rules of order:

United States Volleyball Association Foundation
Presiding: Wilbur H. Peck, President
Recording: Joseph B. Sharpless, Secretary

Attendance and Apologies

1. Call to Order and Opening Remarks	Mr. Peck
2. Certification of Trustees	Mr. Sharpless
3. Review and Approval of Agenda	Mr. Sharpless
4. Approval of Minutes, 2004 Annual Meeting	Mr. Sharpless
5. Treasurer's/Financial Report	Mr. Wendelboe
6. Grant Requests/Status of Approved Grants	Dr. Beal, Chair
7. Fund Raising	Ms. Mara (USAV Staff)
8. Activity Report: STARS Heritage Club	Mr. Peck
9. Assignments: Tasks and Committees	Mr. Peck
10. Election of Trustees, Class of 2006	Ms. Viera, Chair
11. Election of Officers, 2004 – 2005	Ms. Viera, Chair
12. Old Business	
a. Starlings; Coaches Forum	Ms. Howard
b. Other	
13. New Business	
a. Discussion: Development of Policy/Guidelines for Grant Requests	Mr. Dunn
14. Adjournment and Next meeting	

Glossary

Ad hoc committee – assigned for specific purpose(s)

Example: Membership incentives committee for Women's Basketball Coaches Association (WBCA) or Collegiate Football Coaches Association (CFCA); this committee's goal is to collect information about increasing membership of the organization and present a report, including a plan to implement recommendations made by the committee to the board.

Amend – to change or revise a law, bill, etc.

Amendment – a revision or change proposed or made in a bill, law, etc.

Ballot – a ticket, paper, etc. by which a vote is registered

Board – a group of administrators; council

Chair – an important or official position; a person who presides over a meeting

Commission – a group of people assigned to perform specified duties

Committee – a group of people chosen to report or act upon a certain matter

Debate – a discussion of opposing reasons

Executive Summary – a brief report covering the main points of a larger document. It includes purpose, problem, solution, rationale, and recommendations.

Majority (simple majority) – the greater number

Example: Of the 24 board members, 13 constitute a majority (simple majority).

Majority vote (simple majority vote) - the number by which the votes cast for the candidate who receives more than half the votes, exceed the sum of all the other votes cast

Example: Of 24 board members, 13 yes votes constitute a majority (simple majority).

Minority – the lesser number

Example: Of 24 board members, less than 12 constitute a minority.

Motion – a proposal formally made in a meeting

Parliamentarian – a person who is skilled in parliamentary rules and who is designated as the official interpreter of those rules

Parliamentary procedures – established rules that governs the operation of the organization

Point of order – a way to temporarily suspend debate when a situation becomes disorderly.

Example: The chair can declare Point of Order when a member becomes emotional, perhaps shouting.

Postpone – to put off until later; delay

Preamble – an introduction to a constitution, which contains the name of the committee and names of the members, the mission, and a review of procedures.

President – the highest executive officer of an organization, generally elected

Proposed solution – idea put forth for consideration and approval

Quorum – the minimum amount of members required to be present before an assembly can transact business

Example: On a 24-member board, a simple majority must be present in order to conduct business. This would mean that 13 of the members would have to be present for a quorum to exist.

Rationale – used in a report to substantiate reasons why statements are included

Rescind – to revoke or cancel

Restrictions – what an organization is limited to in scope

Roll call – the reading aloud of a roll to find out who is present and who is absent

Second – a formal endorsement of a motion by a voting member at a meeting

Secretary – person who keeps records, handles correspondence, etc. for an organization

Subcommittee – a small committee chosen from a main committee

Example: A subcommittee was formed to complete one of many smaller tasks as determined by the chair of the main committee.

Task force – a group assigned to a complete a specific task

Treasurer – an officer in charge of a treasury, as of an organization

Vice President – an officer next in rank to the president, acting during the absence of the President

Vote – a decision on a proposal

References

Hums, M.A. & MacLean, J.C. (2004). *Governance and policy in sport organizations*. Scottsdale, AZ: Holcomb Hathaway, Publishers.

Robert's rules of order newly revised. (2000). 10th ed. Cambridge, MA: Perseus Publishing.

Robert, H. M. (1915). Public domain. *Robert's rules of order revised*. www.constitution.org/rror/rror--00.htm

Utter, E.C. (1949). *Parliamentary law at a glance*. Chicago: Contemporary Books.

www.roberts-rules.com

SPORT GOVERNANCE: A WEBLIOGRAPHY

A search for Internet sources was undertaken on the topic of sport governance, administration and management to elicit
I. full text documents,
II. practices or policies of associations.
III. college and university courses
IV. software

The documents and sources listed below have many similar characteristics and express the fundamental organizational management philosophies including:

- clear-cut principles of administration and management of sports organizations
- essential organizational policy analysis, design and implementation
- accountability in financial and other matters
- statements on insuring fairness in all competitions
- advancing sporting excellence from grass roots participation through to service provision for high performance athletes

I. FULL TEXT PAPERS AND DOCUMENTS

Code of governance for national sports associations,
(To find this document, use key words *code governance* in Site Search box)
Singapore, Singapore Sports Council, 2003.
http://www.ssc.gov.sg/

Corporate governance issues in a professional sport, by Julie A. Foreman, Hawthorn, Vic: School of Business, Swinburne University of Technology, *ca* 2001, 19p.
http://www.commerce.adelaide.edu.au/apira/papers/Foreman172.pdf

Findings of officers and legal counsel: sport governance,
Lexington, KY: USA Equestrian, July 3, 2002, 3p.
http://www.equestrian.org/EquestrianGovernance/sports-governance/findings-sport-governance.pdf

Game Plan: a strategy for delivering Government's sport and physical activity objectives,
London: Prime Minister's Strategy Unit, December 2002, 32p.
http://www.number-10.gov.uk/su/sport/report/01.htm

Governance in sport: draft – statement of good governance principles for sports governing bodies, by Herbert Smith. A draft statement prepared by the Governance in Sport Committee for discussion at a conference ...in Brussels, 26-27th February 2001, 6p.
http://www.governance-in-sport.com/

Governance in Sport, Canberra: Australian Sports Commission, 2002, *ca* 6p. (See this and other documents in 2002 list of full text documents)
http://www.ausport.gov.au/fulltext/

Governance and Sport: resource guide, by Dr. David Hindley, Nottingham Trent University, [for the Learning and Teaching Support Network on Hospitality, Leisure, Sport and Tourism] c2003, 8p.
http://www.hlst.ltsn.ac.uk/resources/governance.html

Report of the Independent Soccer Inquiry, David Crawford, Chair, Canberra: Australian Sports Commission, 2003, 89p. (in PDF format)
http://www.soccerinquiry.org.au/report.htm
    This Review committee is examining the existing governance, management and structure of soccer in Australia and recommending changes.

Sport governance and European integration, by Luca Barani
In, [proceedings] of the European Union Studies Association Biennial Conference, 8th, March 27-29, 2003, Nashville, Tennessee. 31p. (Available to registered users i.e. Members of the EUSA that is headquartered at the University of Pittsburgh:
http://www.eustudies.org

II. Associations, Institutes, Councils
European Association for Sport Management
http://web.tiscali.it/no-redirect-tiscali/easmorg/

Football Governance Research Centre, University of London at Birkbeck
(based at the Clore Management Centre in central London)
http://www.football-research.org/
> This institute's focus is on management-related research on
> professional football (soccer). In the Research and Publications
> section are many full text documents available in PDF format, e.g.
> *The State of the Game: Corporate Governance of Football Clubs
> 2002* (516 KB)

North American Society for Sport Management
http://www.nassm.com/
> NASSMs periodical, Journal of sport management is published by
> Human Kinetics and is indexed in SPORTDiscus

Sport Management Association of Australia & New Zealand
http://www.gu.edu.au/school/lst/services/smaanz/home.html

Youth Sports Research Council, Rutgers University
http://youthsports.rutgers.edu/
> The YSRC, in cooperation with the New Jersey Recreation and Park
> Association have created a task force of individuals who administer
> outstanding youth sport programs and are in the process of identifying
> the "Core Elements" of quality programs in youth sports. On their
> website is the full text of the Guidelines for Recreational Youth Sport
> Agencies: a Youth Sport Charter that describes the goals and
> principles of excellent youth sport management (see
> http://youthsports.rutgers.edu/youth_sports_charter.html)

III. SELECTED UNIVERSITY COURSES ON SPORT GOVERNANCE
The following course outlines show what is being taught in universities.
Most have bibliographies attached.

Sport Governance & Ethics 412 (2002), taught by James Reese, Ohio
University, Institute for Applied and Professional Ethics. (Click on Sport
Governance in list on left hand side)
http://freud.citl.ohiou.edu/ethics/materials.php?records=9

Sport Governance, SPM 2113, Edith Cowan University, School of Management
http://www.business.ecu.edu.au/info/current/outlines/spm2113.pdf

Management and Governance of Sport and Leisure, Research Themes in the Institute of Sport and Leisure Policy, Loughborough University, UK
http://www.lboro.ac.uk/departments/sscs/institutes/salp/mangov.html

SOMIT – Sport Organization Management Interactive Teaching & Learning, Swiss Virtual Campus, supported by IDHEAP Lausanne University (project leader), Fribourg University, Berne University, UASS Macolin, Swiss Olympic Association.
http://www.virtualcampus.ch/display.php?lang=1&pname=991018pres

- The SOMIT project consists of creating interactive distance learning in sport organization management and consists of 60 hours per semester. It is aimed at graduate students enrolled in Swiss universities.

IV. SOFTWARE
The metasearch of the Internet also elicited a company website called Clublink. This company from Montreal, Quebec sells national club and organization management software specifically created for sport clubs, governing bodies and divisions.
http://www.integratedsports.net/

BIBLIOGRAPHY — BOOKS AND ARTICLES

Abrams, J. (1996). *Organizational change in national governing bodies of sport.* Leeds, Great Britain: Leeds Metropolitan University, Sports Council.

Baxter, V. (1990). The National Collegiate Athletics Association and the governance of higher education. *The Sociological Quarterly, 31,* 403-421.

Brackenridge, C. (1996). *Child protection in sport-policies, procedures and systems: Report of a sports council seminar for national governing bodies.* Cheltenham, MA: Cheltenham & Gloucester College of Higher Education, Sports Council.

Brown, A. (2000). European football and the European Union: Governance, participation and social cohesion towards a policy research agenda. *Soccer and Society, 1*(2), 129-150.

Cao, K. & Liu, X. (1998). Transformation of sport policy in Britain. *Journal of Xi'an Institute of Physical Education, 15,* 13-16, 50.

Chalip, L. (1995). Policy analysis in sport management. *Journal of Sport Management, 9*(1), 1-13.

Chalip, L. (1996). Critical policy analysis: The Illustrative case of New Zealand sport policy development. *Journal of Sport Management, 10,* 310-324.

Cohen, G. (ed.). (2000). *Women in sport: Issues and controversies* (2nd ed.) Oxon Hill, MD: NAGWS/AAHPERD Publications.

Corbett, R. & Findlay, H.A. (1999). *Good policies, good governance: A guide for sport organizations.* Ottawa, Canada: Centre for Sport and Law.

Crumley, B., Kirwin, J. & Sautter, U. (2000). Football's crewe cut: Seeking an end to transfer fees, the European Commission tackles soccer's governing bodies. *Time International, 156,* 93.

Darby, P. (2000). Africa's place in FIFAs global order: A theoretical framework. *Soccer and Society, 1*(2), 36-61.

Davies, J. & Mabin, V. (2000). Assessing the relative effectiveness of sports organizations: A case study reviewing an application of MCDA in sport. *European Journal for Sport Management, 7*(1), 56-81.

Evans, J., Davis, B. & Penney, D. (1997). Making progress: Sports policy, women and innovation in physical education. *European Journal of Physical Education, 2,* 39-50.

Gardiner, S. (ed.). (2001). Governance of sport: National, European and international perspectives, in *Sports Law* (2nd ed). London, England: Cavendish publishers.

Henry, I.P. & Theodorsaki, E.I. (1994). Organizational structures and contexts in British national governing bodies of sport. *International Review for the Sociology of Sport, 29*(3), 243-268.

Houlihan, B. (2000). Sporting excellence, schools and sports development: The politics of crowded policy spaces. *European Physical Education Review, 6,* 171-193.

Hunter, R.J. & Mayo, A. M. (1999). The business of sport. *Mid-Atlantic Journal of Business, 35*(2-3), 75-76

Inglis, S. (1997). Shared leadership in the governance of amateur sport: Perceptions of executive directors and volunteer board members. *Avante, 13*(1), 14-33.

Kikulis, L. M. (2000). Continuity and change in governance and decision making in national sport organizations: Institutional explanations. *Journal of Sport Management, 14*(4), 293-320.

Kluka, D. (Ed). (2000). *Women, sport, and physical activity: Sharing good practice.* Schondorf, Germany: ICSSPE/Verlag Karl Hofman GmbH & Co.

Kluka, D. & Schilling, G. (Eds). (2001). *The business of sport.* Berlin, Germany: ICSSPE/Meyer & Meyer Verlag.

Li, M. (2000). Regulation of elite sport in the United States. *International Sports Journal, 4*(2), 26-43.

Ma, X (1997). The past, present and future of Hong Kong sport. *Sports Science, 17,* 10-18.

Papadimitriou, D. (1999). Voluntary boards of directors in Greek sport governing bodies. *European Journal for Sport Management, 6,* 78-103.

Stevens, J. (2000). Reinventing sport governing bodies: A conceptual framework analysis. *Avante, 6,* 82-94.

Stier, W.F., Jr. (1993). *Education, Women and the Olympics.* (ERIC Document Reproduction Service No. ED351300).

Stier, W.F., Jr. (1991). Women in the Olympic movement: Advancing women's roles through education. *Journal of Physical Education, Recreation and Dance, 62*(9), 62-66.

Sugden, J. & Tomlinson, A. (1998). Power and resistance in the governance of world football: Theorizing FIFAs transnational impact. *Journal of Sport and Social Issues, 23*(3), 299-316.

Thoma, J. E. & Chalip, L. (1996). *Sport governance in the global community*. Morgantown, West Virginia: Fitness Information Technology, Inc.

Welch, S. (2001, March 2). NCAA creates panel to review its governance structure. *The Chronicle of Higher Education, 47*(25), A-44.

Wilcox, R. C. (1994). *Sport in the Global Village*. Morgantown, West Virginia: Fitness Information Technology, Inc.

Zhao, B., Cai, J., Li, L., Li, W., Bao, M. & Zhou, W. (1997). Study on the policy system for sport industry in China. *Sports Science, 17*, 1-7.

ASSESSMENT TOOL FOR COMPLIANCE: SOUTH AFRICAN EXAMPLE

1. Official name of National Sport Federation
2. What is your current position within the Federation
Ordinary individually registered member (e.g. Athlete / Coach / Official / Supporter)
Member of Executive Board / Management Board / Executive Committee
Member of other committee (e.g. Technical / Administrative / Financial)
Part-time paid employee / Staff Member of National Federation
Full-time paid employee / Staff member of National Federation
Volunteer
3. Estimated number of people participating in sport
4. Number of Members serving on Executive Board / Committee
5. Did the Federation have an election to elect new Management members during the past 24 months?
6. Number of Management sub-committees dealing specifically with technical/sport and / or training related matters (i.e. coaching / high performance etc)?
7. Total number of individuals collectively serving on committees identified in 6. (total number of people on these committees combined)?
8. Number of Management sub-committees dealing specifically with non-technical matters (i.e. financial / marketing / CSR etc.)?
9. Total number of individuals collectively serving on these non-technical committees combined number of people of all non-technical committees)?
10. How many provincial or regional bodies / association are registered or affiliated to the Federation?
11. Does the Federation have a Website?
12. Does the Federation have a formal written ethics policy?

Ranking from Yes/Strongly Agree to No/Strongly Disagree

The Federation fulfils a corporate social responsibility (CSR) towards society	1	2	3	4	5
Management is committed to principles of good governance	1	2	3	4	5
Outsiders can easily obtain a true picture of the current state of affairs of the Federation	1	2	3	4	5
The role of the Federation is only to draw up and codify the rules of the sport	1	2	3	4	5
Existing procedures to resolve differences are easily accessible by members of the Federation	1	2	3	4	5
Roles and responsibilities of all assemblies, committees and commissions (e.g. disciplinary committees / financial oversight committee etc) have been taken up into a written document	1	2	3	4	5
This Federation acts in a non-discriminatory and non-exploitative manner towards people within society in general	1	2	3	4	5
The maximum duration any individual can serve on any non-executive committee is fixed	1	2	3	4	5

Information on the Federation and its managerial and financial activities are available on the company website (if the Federation does not have website, circle 1)	1	2	3	4	5
All decisions and actions taken can be substantiated by means of sufficient reasoning (justified and reasoned to be in the best interest of the Federation and its members)	1	2	3	4	5
Accountability is not abdicated by various role players (e.g. Management accepts accountability for poor administration of the Federations affairs)	1	2	3	4	5
Management has an acute awareness of, and commitment to the underlying principles of good governance	1	2	3	4	5
There is a commitment by Management to adhere to behavior that is universally deemed correct, acceptable and proper	1	2	3	4	5
No stakeholder group can exercise enough power to influence the objectivity of decisions taken by management	1	2	3	4	5
Decisions are taken with cognizance of the effect it will have on all interest groups	1	2	3	4	5
Clear accountability can be assigned to those who make decisions	1	2	3	4	5
A direct and open communication channel exists between Management and all individual Federation members (individuals have a direct and open way to communicate with Management)	1	2	3	4	5
Contingency plans exist (and will be implemented) to keep the Federation on course if necessary	1	2	3	4	5
There is a clear distinction made between the Federation's formal management function versus the pursuit of activities for financial gain, to ensure that a conflict of interest does not arise	1	2	3	4	5
Management accepts full accountability for failed actions or decisions	1	2	3	4	5
Elections of Management members are conducted in a free and fair manner	1	2	3	4	5
A written statement of the Federation's responsibilities is readily available to members	1	2	3	4	5
Management assumes accountability for failed actions and mismanagement	1	2	3	4	5
Management remains accountable for the financial success of the Federation	1	2	3	4	5
Management is available to answer any questions and queries from all legitimate stakeholders	1	2	3	4	5
Decisions and policies are free from undue outside influences	1	2	3	4	5
Regard for environmental and human rights issues will lead to economic and monetary benefits for the Federation	1	2	3	4	5
Fund distribution is done in an objective and justifiable manner	1	2	3	4	5
Existing procedures to resolve differences are efficient	1	2	3	4	5
The Federation is managed in a financially responsible manner	1	2	3	4	5
There is no ambiguity in terms of voting rights and eligibility of members	1	2	3	4	5
A large percentage of information within the Federation is not deemed confidential	1	2	3	4	5
Management regularly makes information and data available to the press and general public	1	2	3	4	5
Management does not interfere when a dispute between a member and the Federation is referred for arbitration	1	2	3	4	5
Principles of good governance are consistently enforced	1	2	3	4	5
An open tender system is in place and documented	1	2	3	4	5
Sound procurement policies are in place and well documented	1	2	3	4	5
There is a general high level of adherence to ethical standards within the Federation	1	2	3	4	5
Rights and benefits are given to members and stakeholder groups according to	1	2	3	4	5

their relative level of influence and importance					
The interests of all members and stakeholders are taken into account when decisions are made	1	2	3	4	5
Committee / Management members seldom find themselves in a position where a conflict of interest could arise	1	2	3	4	5
Details such as the identity and qualifications of each serving management member, are readily available to members and outside stakeholders	1	2	3	4	5
Decisions taken by Management are highly objective	1	2	3	4	5
Decisions taken by non-management committees are highly objective	1	2	3	4	5
The details of nominated individuals are made available well before elections take place	1	2	3	4	5
There is regular communication on the state of the Federation's finances and financial activities to members and other stakeholders	1	2	3	4	5
The Federation is responsible only for those individuals directly involved in the sport	1	2	3	4	5
Relevant information regarding the Federation is shared with all stakeholders	1	2	3	4	5
Accountability for the entire Federation and its members, ultimately lies with Management	1	2	3	4	5
Policies, decisions, election results and other matters are regularly communicated to members and stakeholders	1	2	3	4	5
Formal election procedures are set out in writing and communicated in advance to all members eligible to vote during Federation elections	1	2	3	4	5
A procedure is in place to resolving differences between either management, management and members or between members per se	1	2	3	4	5
Differences as described above can be easily resolved through external appeals or arbitration	1	2	3	4	5
A clear chain of responsibility and accountability exists within the hierarchical structure of the organization	1	2	3	4	5
The Federation's corporate social responsibility is well defined	1	2	3	4	5
Existing procedures to resolve differences adhere to the requirements of transparency	1	2	3	4	5
The Federation has a responsibility to act responsibly towards environmental issues	1	2	3	4	5
Management ultimately assumes responsibility for the Federation and its members	1	2	3	4	5
All members have the same legitimate rights within the Federation	1	2	3	4	5
All members are treated equally within the Federation	1	2	3	4	5
During Management decisions, objectivity is sought to ensure that no discrimination of any kind prevails	1	2	3	4	5
General reports on the state of the organization are made available in a candid, accurate and timely fashion to stakeholders	1	2	3	4	5
Existing measures and mechanisms are sufficient to avoid potential conflicts of interest	1	2	3	4	5
Frequent reports aimed at the needs of specific stakeholders (e.g. Government, Sponsors) are made available	1	2	3	4	5
Clear guidelines exist for the handling of all legitimate stakeholders (e.g. activists, media) and members interests	1	2	3	4	5
The sole responsibility of the Federation is the development and promotion of the popularity and support of the sport	1	2	3	4	5
A clear statement of the Federation's formal approach to governance has been communicated to members and other stakeholders	1	2	3	4	5
The current structure of the Federation facilitates effective management	1	2	3	4	5

Decisions are taken in the best interests of the Federation as a whole	1	2	3	4	5
Mismanagement by a member of Management is adequately penalized	1	2	3	4	5
The organization responds well to external social issues	1	2	3	4	5
The organization responds well to internal social issues	1	2	3	4	5
The current structure of the Federation contributes to effective management of the Federation	1	2	3	4	5
The appointed auditors are independent and unbiased	1	2	3	4	5
Decisions are not biased towards any specific interest, stakeholder or member grouping	1	2	3	4	5
Administration of funds is transparent, accountable and objective	1	2	3	4	5
Existing procedures to resolve differences adhere to the requirements of procedural fairness	1	2	3	4	5
Directives with regard to voting rights and procedures are clearly communicated to all members	1	2	3	4	5
Different committees have been established with clearly defined responsibilities in terms of performing various organizational functions	1	2	3	4	5
All members are treated with the same level of respect and tolerance	1	2	3	4	5
There are examination procedures to assess the accuracy and truthfulness of nominated individuals' curriculum vitae	1	2	3	4	5
The maximum duration any individual can serve on the executive board is fixed	1	2	3	4	5
The Federation own a website which is regularly updated	1	2	3	4	5
The Federation's website contains all relevant information which pertains to the daily running and management of the Federation	1	2	3	4	5
The Federation has comprehensive and detailed ethical policy which deals with most or all possible matters pertaining to ethical conduct that might arise	1	2	3	4	5
The duration of the serving term of elected officials is documented	1	2	3	4	5

SUPPORTING DOCUMENTS: EXAMPLES
WOMEN IN SPORT

The Brighton Declaration Of Principles

Women, Sport, and the Challenge of Change, the first international conference on women and sport, brought together national and international policy and decision makers in Brighton, UK, May 5-8, 1994. From that conference came the Brighton Declaration, a statement of principles designed to accelerate change and redress the imbalances women face in their participation and involvement in sport.

THE PRINCIPLES

1. Equity and Equality in Society and Sport

a. Every effort should be made by state and government machineries to ensure that institutions and organizations responsible for sport comply with the equality provisions of the Charter of the United Nations, the Universal Declaration of Human Rights and the UN Convention on the Elimination of All Forms of Discrimination Against Women.

b. Equal opportunity to participate and be involved in sport whether for the purpose of leisure and recreation, health promotion or high performance, is the right of every woman, regardless of race, color, language, religion, creed, sexual orientation, age, marital status, disability, political belief or affiliation, national or social origin.

c. Resources, power and responsibility should be allocated fairly and without discrimination on the basis of sex, but such allocation should redress any inequitable balance in the benefits available to women and men.

2. Facilities
Women's participation in sport is influenced by the extent, variety, and accessibility of facilities. The planning, design and management of these facilities should appropriately and equitably meet the particular needs of women in the community, with special attention given to the need for childcare provision and safety.

3. School and Junior Sport
Research demonstrates that girls and boys approach sport from markedly different perspectives. Those responsible for sport, education, recreation, and physical education of young people should ensure that an equitable range of opportunities and learning experience, which accommodate the values, attitudes and aspirations of girls, is incorporated in programs to develop physical fitness and basic sport skills of young people.

4. Developing Participation
Women's participation in sport is influenced by the range of activities available. Those responsible for delivering sporting opportunities and programs should provide and promote activities, which meet women's needs and aspirations.

5. High Performance Sport
a. Governments and sports organizations should provide equal opportunity to women to reach their sports performance potential by ensuring that all activities and programs relating to performance improvements take account of the specific needs of female athletes.
b. Those supporting elite and/or professional athletes should ensure that competition opportunities, rewards, incentives. recognition. sponsorship, promotion, and other forms of support are provided fairly and equitably to both women and men.

6. Leadership in Sport
Women are under-represented in the leadership and decision-making of all sport and sport-related organizations. Those responsible for these areas should develop policies and programs and design structures which increase the number of women coaches, advisors, decision makers, officials, administrators and sports personnel at all levels with special attention given to recruitment, development, and retention.

7. Education, Training, and Development

Those responsible for the education, training and development of coaches and other sports personnel should ensure that education processes and experiences address issues relating to gender equity and the needs of female athletes, equitably reflect women's role in sport and take account of women's leadership experiences, values and attitudes.

8. Sports Information and Research

Those responsible for research and providing information on sport should develop policies and programs to increase knowledge and understanding about women and sport and ensure that research norms and standards are based on research on women and men.

9. Resources

Those responsible for the allocation of resources should ensure that support is available for sportswomen, women's programs and special measures to advance this Declaration of Principles.

10.   Domestic and International Co-operation

Government and non-government organizations should incorporate the promotion of issues of gender equity and the sharing of examples of good practice in women and sport policies and programs in their associations with other organizations, within both domestic and international arenas.

The Windhoek Call for Action

The 2nd World Conference on Women and Sport was held in Windhoek, Namibia, 19-22 May 1998. The Call for Action is addressed to all men and women who are responsible for, or who directly influence the conduct, development or promotion of sport, or who are in any way involved in the employment, education, management, training, development or care of girls and women in sport. In addition to re-affirming the principles of the Brighton Declaration, the Conference delegates called for action in the following areas:

1. Develop action plans with objectives and targets to implement the principles of the Brighton Declaration, and monitor and report upon their implementation.
2. Reach out beyond the current boundaries of the sport sector to the global women's equality movement and develop closer partnerships between sport and women's organizations on the one side, and representatives from sectors such as education, youth, health, human rights and employment on the other. Develop strategies that help other sectors obtain their objectives through the medium of sport and at the same time further sport objectives.
3. Promote and share information about the positive contribution that girls' and women's involvement in sport makes to social, health and economic issues.
4. Build the capacity of women as leaders and decision-makers and ensure that women play meaningful and visible roles in sport at all levels. Create mechanisms that ensure that young women have a voice in the development of policies and programs that affect them.
5. Avert the "world crisis in physical education" by establishing and strengthening quality physical education programs as key means for the positive introduction to young girls of the skills and other benefits they can acquire through sport. Further, create policies and mechanisms that ensure progression from school to community-based activity.
6. Encourage the media to positively portray and significantly cover the breadth, depth, quality and benefits of girls' and women's involvement in sport.

7. Ensure a safe and supportive environment for girls and women participating in sport at all levels by taking steps to eliminate all forms of harassment and abuse, violence and exploitation, and gender testing.
8. Ensure that policies and programs provide opportunities for all girls and women in full recognition of the differences and diversity among them - including such factors as race, ability, age, religion, sexual orientation, ethnicity, language, culture or their status as an indigenous person.
9. Recognize the importance of governments to sport development and urge them to conduct gender impact analyses and to develop appropriate Legislation, public policy and funding that ensures gender equality in all aspects of sport.
10. Ensure that Official Development Assistance programs provide equal opportunities for girls' and women's development and recognize the potential of sport to achieve development objectives.
11. Encourage more women to become researchers in sport, and more research to be undertaken on critical issues relating to women in sport.

Manila Declaration

FOREWORD

It is in the interest of equality, development and peace that a commitment be made by governmental, non-governmental organizations and all those institutions involved in sport to apply the Principles set out in this Declaration, by developing appropriate policies, structures and mechanisms which:

- ensure that all women and girls have the opportunity to participate in sport in a safe and supportive environment which preserves the rights and dignity of and respect for the individual;
- increase the involvement of women in sport at all levels and in all functions and roles;
- ensure that the knowledge, experience and values of women contribute to the development of sport; and in all functions and roles;
- promote the recognition by women of the intrinsic values of sport and its contribution to personal development and healthy lifestyle. (Adopted from the Brighton Declaration on Women & Sport, 1994)

RESOLUTIONS

RESOLVE that: Equal opportunity to participate and be involved in sport, whether for the purpose of leisure and recreation, health promotion or high performance, be recognized as the right of every girl & women, regardless of race, color, language, religion, creed, gender/sexual orientation, age, marital status, disability, political belief or affiliation, national or social origin.

RESOLVE that: Government and Non-governmental Sports Organizations provide equal opportunities to women to reach their sport performance potential by ensuring that all activities and programs relating to performance improvement take account of the specific needs of female athletes.

RESOLVE that: Those supporting mass-based elite, and/or professional athletes ensure that competition opportunities, reward, incentives, recognition, sponsorship, promotion and other forms of support are provided fairly and equitably to women.
RESOLVE that: Those responsible for the allocation of resources ensure that support is available to sportswomen and women's sport programs.

RESOLVE that: The planning. and management of sport facilities should appropriately and equitably meet the particular needs of women in their respective communities.

RESOLVE that: Policies be set to ensure greater involvement of women in developing programs and designing structures which would increase the number of women coaches, advisers, decision makers, officials, administrators and sport recruitment, development and retention.

RESOLVE that: Those responsible for the education, scientific training and development of coaches and other sport personnel ensure that educational processes or experiences, address issues relating to gender equity and the needs of female athletes.

RESOLVE that: Those responsible for research and information on sport develop policies and programs to increase knowledge and understanding of women and sport, and ensure that norms and standards are based on research on women.

RESOLVE that: Resources, power and responsibility be allocated fairly and without discrimination on the basis of sex.

RESOLVE that: Government and non-government organizations provide adequate financial support to all sports program for women.

RESOLVE that: An annual Women's Physical Fitness and Sport Week be declared from March 1-8.
RESOLVE that: An International Sports Centre for Women be established in the Asia-Pacific region to serve as a training, research, and information centre as well as resource for study grants and cultural exchange program to the world-wide community.

RESOLVE that: A regular Asia-Pacific Conference be held under the leadership of ICHPER-SD, in co-ordination with the ICHPER-SD Girls and Women Sports Commission.

RESOLVE that: State and government machineries be enjoined to comply with the equality provisions of the Charter of the United Nations, the Universal Declaration of Human Rights and the U.N. Convention, on the Elimination of All Forms of Discrimination against Women.

The Recommendations of the International Conference on Women's Sports for Peace and Development Kathmandu, Nepal, 18-19 November 2004

The following conclusions and recommendations were unanimously accepted by the International Conference in its concluding session.

The Conference recognizes the importance of the education system in socialization and therefore:

i)   recommends a review of the structure and delivery of the physical education system be undertaken in order to develop a gender appropriate curriculum;

ii)   recommends that physical education be incorporated as a compulsory subject in the curriculum of primary, lower secondary and secondary school levels;

iii) recommends that at all levels teachers delivering physical education should have specialist training and that such training should incorporate gender appropriate pedagogical practices. This has implications both for university initial teacher training and for in-service training.

iv)   recommends that a major campaign be launched to promote women's involvement at all levels and in all roles in sport among parents and communities.

The Conference also recognizes the importance of women undertaking leadership roles in sporting organizations at local, national, and international levels. Specifically the conference recommends:

i)   that leadership training courses and seminars be developed for prospective women leaders;

ii)   that the norms proposed by the International Olympic Committee for National Olympic Committees and International Sports Federations, be adopted for appropriate national and local organizations in Nepal, such as the National Olympic Committee, the National Federations and the Sports Council;

iii) that recruitment strategies for attracting prospective women leaders in sport take account of the importance of encouragement by senior figures, particularly women, to foster interest and confidence among potential candidates.

The Conference recognizes that to promote equitable participation for men and women, action should be taken in relation to:

i)   the promotion of appropriate Nepali sportswomen as role models through the media;

ii)   the fostering of indigenous sports activities, and the introduction in Nepal of Women's Netball, one of the few female only sports;

iii) the encouragement of national sports federations to develop strategic proposals to increase women's participation in their particular sport.

Fourth International Conference of Ministers and Senior Officials Responsible for Physical Education and Sport

MINEPS IV
Athens, Greece, 6-8 December 2004
COMMISSION III
WOMEN AND SPORT
RECOMMENDATIONS

INTRODUCTION

- *Affirming* the importance and relevance of previous achievements and work on promoting opportunities for women in and through sport and physical education, Commission III **recognizes** the need to build upon measures made under the auspices of UNESCO – the UNESCO Charter on Sport and Physical Education 1978, the Declaration of Punta del Este (MINEPS III) and the Athens Declaration 2003, – as well as the Brighton Declaration 1994, the Windhoek Call for Action 1998 and the Montreal Communiqué of 2002; the IOC Declaration and targets for at least 20% of women in decision-making positions in NOCs and international federations by 2005;
- *Welcoming* the 2005 International Year of Sport and Physical Education (IYSPE) proclaimed by the United Nations, **urges** all Member States, when developing programs of activity for IYSPE, to take into account the needs of women and girls, to ensure inclusion of all; and to consider the particular role of Olympic education in promoting good values and interest in sport and physical education;
- *Emphasizing* the role of sport and physical education as tools for development, **recognizes** their critical role in achieving the goals of Education for All and the Millennium Development Goals;
- *Recognizing and emphasizing* the crucial role of sport and physical education in the lives and development of women and girls, especially for promoting health, self-esteem and self-confidence, *encouraging* participation and achievement in education, and *promoting* social cohesion and inclusion in social and community life, the Commission made the following recommendations:

1. *Taking into account* the significant work that has already been done to improve the status of women and sport and the desirability for all to share and celebrate these achievements and resources, and
   Acknowledging the generous offer of the Greek Ministry of Sport to provide the financial and human resources to support the development and maintenance of a web-based observatory on women, sport and physical education, to be established under the aegis of UNESCO, Commission III **recommends**:
   - that a Steering Group comprised of officials from the Greek Government, UNESCO and representatives of key international bodies with a mandate in women and sport, meet with a view to preparing a concrete project description for presentation to UNESCO by the end of August 2005;
   - that officials of the Greek Government chair the Steering Group and assume responsibility for a plan and budget for its work.
2. *Having heard* with interest the action of the Finnish Minister to set up a Working Group to develop methods of assessing the impact of legislation, budgeting, distribution of subsidies, etc., on gendered opportunities, **recommends** that governments and NGOs recognize the use of the sport budget as an instrument of gender equality. The Commission also **recommends** the development of a common framework for countries to use self-assessment to monitor progress and to promote the sharing of experiences and skills.
3. *Recognizing* the need for clear evidence and data to support strategies to increase investment in programs to promote opportunities for women and girls in sport and physical education, **recommends** to Member States and to national and international NGOs, that resources be found for programs of research to outline the situation in countries, to ensure more systematic collection of data and to support advocacy in this area, which can be shared between countries and regions of the world.
4. *Recognizing* the importance of the work and recommendations of Commission II on physical education and sport in schools for the systematic development of the skills and confidence for life-long participation in physical activity, especially for girls, Commission III **supports its recommendations** that sufficient time be found in the curriculum to deliver physical education to children – all girls and boys, whatever their particular needs.

This crucial role should also be emphasized through UNESCO's own Associated Schools Network **(ASP)**, so that the wider benefits of curricular physical education can be demonstrated, especially for girls throughout their lives.

5. *Stressing* the particular barrier facing women in countries without sufficient numbers of trained women personnel, and where it is desirable or even essential that women and girls are led by women, **supports the recommendation** of Tunisia that UNESCO discuss with partner organizations such as the International Council of Sport Science and Physical Education and the International Olympic Committee, means of facilitating appropriate training for women, especially in least developed countries (LDCs), for elementary school physical education, coaching, officiating and administration.

6. *Acknowledging* the world-wide challenges of the growth of childhood obesity, especially among girls; high incidences of early sexual activity and teenage pregnancy; and osteoporosis among post-menopausal women, and the significant role of physical activity and exercise in combating these, **recommends** to Member States that intervention programs should be developed to address these challenges, with appropriate systems of monitoring outcomes.

7. *Appreciating* the role of traditional games, sports and dance in the development of opportunities for activity for girls and women, and for continuity of culture and using sport as a tool for development, Commission III **recommends** that Member States with programs of development in this area refer to TAFISA, the international NGO whose role is to promote and share experience of traditional games, sports and dance.

8. *Recognizing and celebrating* the contributions made by women to the promotion of opportunities for sport and physical education for people with special needs, and for people who are excluded from mainstream provision; and in view of men's relatively low participation in these areas, **recommends** that Member States and NGOs consider ways of increasing the number of men taking part in such work.

9. **Invites** Member States to support the recommendation of Japan to send at least one delegate to the Fourth World Conference on Women and Sport, to be held in Kumamoto, Japan from 11 to 14 May 2006.